WRITING AWAY *the* STIGMA

*Ten Courageous Writers Tell True Stories About Depression,
Bipolar Disorder, ADHD, OCD, PTSD & more*

Edited by **Lee Gutkind** & **Chad Vogler**
Foreword by Joni Schwager

InFACT | BOOKS
Pittsburgh, PA

Rights & Permissions
In Fact Books
c/o Creative Nonfiction Foundation
5501 Walnut Street, Suite 202
Pittsburgh, PA 15232

Telephone: 412-688-0304
Email: information@creativenonfction.org
Website: www.creativenonfiction.org

Cover and book design by Stephen Knezovich
Printed in the United States of America

Additional copies of this book are available through Amazon.com.

CONTENTS

A Common, Treatable Disease

Joni Schwager

MENTAL ILLNESS IS A DISEASE THAT AFFECTS EVERYONE, whether it occurs in the form of personal experience or in the trials of a family member, friend, or colleague. About half of American adults will struggle with some form of mental health problem in their lifetime. Despite the prevalence of mental illness, however, the stigma associated with it continues to rear its ugly head. Few talk publicly about their experiences, and stigma remains a major barrier for individuals and families that might otherwise seek help and access to treatment. Successful evidence-based treatment models (which may or may not involve medication) have been developed, and researchers uncover new information about brain function every day, yet people often blame themselves for their conditions. Embarrassed and ashamed, they struggle to recover from their illnesses without external intervention, as if their medical conditions were personal weaknesses or flaws.

The Staunton Farm Foundation is in the business of offering grants to nonprofit organizations that strive to improve the lives of people with mental illness. The stories you are about to read are the results of a grant awarded to the Creative Nonfiction Foundation for the purpose of developing a writing workshop. Led by founder and editor Lee Gutkind, this fellowship gave its participants the opportunity to tell their stories while learning to write them well. I want to thank the brave people in this book, who are sharing their stories publicly.

The media does us a disservice when they represent the extreme end of the mental illness spectrum as if it were the norm. There are many forms of mental illness, ranging from mild to severe. We know that only 5 to 7 percent of people with mental illness are those with serious or extreme disorders, while the other 93 to 95 percent fall on the continuum somewhere between mild to moderate. To counter the stigma and discrimination shown toward those with mental health and substance disorders, people need to come forward and share their stories. When they do, we recognize ourselves in them, and we can identify and better understand the ways that mental illness affects our lives.

People are speaking out. Every day, celebrities, sports figures, and role models are coming forward and sharing their experiences, and many TV shows and movies now include insightful storylines about mental illness. And we are seeing major shifts in the medical world as well: Primary care practices are adding mental health professionals to their teams, and mental health services are finally on par with physical health in insurance plans. The Affordable Care Act lists mental health as an essential health benefit.

We are making an impact. Many thanks to this project—and again, to the participants—for moving the needle of change a little further in the right direction, helping us to recognize mental illness for what it is: a common, treatable disease.

Writing Away the Stigma
The Workshop, the Rewards, and the Cost

Lee Gutkind

I BELIEVE IN STORIES—TRUE STORIES. And I believe that true stories, told well—the genre known as creative nonfiction—can precipitate action and change. This, after all, is why writers write. We want our work to make a difference, despite the cost.

Despite the cost?

These days, Americans are talking more about the challenges of mental illness. We are not doing much about it as a nation, as of yet, but we are talking—giving it lip service—and that's a step forward. But the stigma remains prevalent.

What is stigma? I think most of us don't know what a powerful word it is, how damning and threatening it is. Look it up! Stigma is defined as a mark of disgrace, shame, dishonor, and humiliation.

Can this be true? Are we disgraceful because we suffer from mental illness? Should we be—do we deserve to be—dishonored? Hardly. Like those who suffer from cancer, diabetes, or heart disease, for example, we do not choose to be diagnosed with mental illness. As they say, you have to learn to play the hand you've been dealt.

Which brings me back to the cost. What will it cost—in reputation, income, professional advancement, friendships—the ten brave writers who have come out to tell their stories of mental illness in this collection? Maybe—hopefully—nothing. But they've put themselves on the line, purposely making themselves and their friends and their families vulnerable for the sake of others who don't yet know how to tell their stories, or who are simply too fearful to do so because of the possible consequences.

By the way, twelve people were initially accepted into the Writing Away the Stigma workshop from which these essays came about, twelve people who committed to telling their stories no matter the consequence. And yet, two of the twelve writers backed out: one at the conclusion of the workshop, and another quite recently, right before this book went into production. Writing away the stigma is a daunting thing to do.

There were eighty-one applicants to the Writing Away the Stigma workshop, a series of five three-hour, once-a-week classes open to residents of a ten-county area in southwestern Pennsylvania. The goal in the end was to write a true story, a creative nonfiction essay, about mental illness—their own, or that of a friend or family member.

I taught the workshops, which were offered free of charge due to the generous support of the Staunton Farm Foundation. We had a public reading a few months after the class ended, and the turnout was amazing: one hundred people from all over the area attended to see the participants stand in front of a microphone, identify themselves, and read excerpts of their work. It was a dramatic and powerful experience—a magic moment of creativity and trust when these survivors and supporters shared their lives with so many strangers.

True stories are powerful persuaders. The more stories told by the voices in the crowd—by the one in four people who will suffer from a diagnosable mental illness this year—the more legislators will listen (and perhaps one day take action); the more employers will open up their hiring parameters; the more Big Pharma will be pressured to lower the outlandish prices of their products; and the more even the experts, the MDs, PhDs, and MSWs, will learn to work together and support one another toward a common goal.

The Writing Away the Stigma workshop and this book are a call to action for those who have suffered in silence to speak out. Now is the time to tell your vivid and unforgettable true stories to anyone who will listen. We must raise a deafening chorus that will be heard throughout the country, striking a chord, compelling action, and eventually forcing a shift toward understanding and appreciation of the challenges presented by mental illness. We must write away the stigma, tell our true stories, until the stigma no longer exists.

Acknowledgements

This collection is the result of a five-part writing workshop that was made possible by generous support from the Staunton Farm Foundation and led by Lee Gutkind, and which took place at the University Club in Pittsburgh in the fall of 2013. The editors are grateful to the participants not only for their remarkable stories, but also for the courage they showed in participating and in allowing their stories to be published here.

Any book is the work of many people. The editors would like to thank, in particular, Matt Spindler and Jamie Beaudoin for their careful fact checking, Robyn Jodlowski for her technical expertise, and Stephen Knezovich for design and layout, as well as everyone at the Creative Nonfiction Foundation and the Staunton Farm Foundation.

The Runaway Bunny

Andrea Laurion

CHILD PSYCHIATRISTS HAVE GREAT TOY COLLECTIONS, and Dr. Gainor was no exception. Despite the variety, I played with the same one during every visit—a white rabbit puppet. At nine years old, I was getting a bit too old for toys, but I quickly decided that the puppet was too cute to pass up.

Dr. Gainor, a short brunette with a motherly vibe, asked me a lot of questions, and as a kid who loved to talk, I didn't mind answering them. Unlike most adults, she seemed to listen. We talked about school and home, mostly, but she'd sometimes ask what I wanted to be when I grew up, or she'd ask what books I liked to read. She also prescribed the little orange pills I had to take every morning and afternoon.

"You know how you wear glasses to see better?" she would say. "These are like glasses for your brain. They help your brain focus."

On one particular visit, she asked my father about his expectations for me.

"I just want her to do well in school," he said. "Get some scholarships, go to college."

I didn't look up, too busy playing with the puppet. I held the bunny to my chest, stroking it gently, pretending that my hand wasn't what kept it alive.

She turned her attention to me. "Did you hear what your dad said?"

"Yep." I ran my fingers over the soft faux fur, the bunny tucked under my chin. Neither of them knew that my heart was breaking

His hope that I would attend college is understandable, now. Any good parent wants to provide the best possible future for his or her child, and maybe fathers like mine, who themselves didn't go to college, feel this desire more than most. But I was a child at the time, and I didn't understand this. He wanted me to be like the kids in my class who got straight As, who sat still at their desks and remembered their scissors on Art Day. What I heard was, "I want her to be perfect," and I knew I never could be.

The little orange pills were to salve an itch I didn't know I had. They made me obedient in the name of normalcy.

"You can't pay attention to anything," my classmates would tell me during group projects, echoing what they'd heard adults say. Actually, I paid attention to everything: a pencil dropping across the room; a dog barking outside; the teacher shuffling papers on her desk. Each little activity drew me away from the task in front of me. It seemed to others as if I couldn't keep my eyes on my math test, when in reality I saw it all.

It was funny to me that I had to take those pills to focus, because when I was really interested in something, I was all in. Especially reading. I couldn't start reading at the end of the school day because I would get so immersed that I wouldn't hear my afternoon bus called over the PA system. When I saw *Star Wars*, a few years later, I completely understood the concept of "light speed." My brain still feels this way when I get super involved in some activity, like reading, writing, or watching a favorite TV show.

But I was also in constant motion. My muscles were never comfortable. I would sit up in my chair, only to realize I needed to scratch my nose. And the hair behind my ears was tangled, so of course I had to run my fingers through it. Now I was sitting back in my seat and crossing my ankles, but my shoes weren't tied as tight as I'd have liked, so I'd better tie them, and—oh no!—I knocked my pencil to the ground. Staying in one place during class was bad. Sitting through Catholic Mass was worse.

"Sit *still*," my Catholic school teachers would growl down at me in the church pew.

"I *am*," I said. I didn't understand the problem. I never stood up once. So I was messing with the hymnals and swinging my feet and picking at the scab on my knee and biting my nails and craning my head to look at all the stained glass windows and making up stories in my head. My butt never left the seat.

The pills made my brain say, "No, don't look up at the kids giggling across the room, this math test is far more interesting." With those pills, I could sit through Mass with my eyes on the priest, watching him at the podium as he talked about Jesus embracing the little children with open arms. When I took those pills, I could be perfect.

When I *took* the pills, of course.

The morning one was easy. My mother was around to bug me until I popped it in my mouth. Afternoons were harder. I had to go to the front office after recess and get it from the secretary, which I forgot to do nearly every day.

"Pardon the interruption," the secretary would call over the loudspeaker. "Andrea Laurion, please report to the office. Andrea Laurion, please report to the office."

I would immediately drop what I was doing, rushing out of class and down the stairs. The pills were kept in a circular plastic case with a collapsible cup. Our plaid skirts didn't come with pockets, so I'd put it in my front shirt pocket when I was done.

"That looks like a can of snuff," one of the girls once said. "Are you doing snuff?"

"No," I answered. "It's for my pill."

I didn't know, yet, that this was something embarrassing. I was honest in the way of children who are unaware that their openness will come back to shame them.

"Don't forget to take your *piiiiill*," some kids called when we walked out to recess.

"Shut up!" I yelled back. Forty-five minutes later, though, I proved them right, as my name echoed through the school's wooden halls. I loved attention, but not this kind—not the kind that made the rest of the school wonder if I was always in trouble.

I grew to hate those pills. I didn't want to be perfect if it meant standing out like this, and I started fighting with my mother about taking them.

"No!" I'd scream. "I don't want to take my pill today!"

She'd bring up Dr. Gainor's glasses analogy. "If you're not going to take your pill, then give me your glasses," she'd say. "Your brain needs these pills like your eyes need your glasses."

Usually this would work, but my dad would join in the screaming matches if I was being pigheaded. And he always won.

"TAKE YOUR PILL!" He'd thunder. "It's that simple!" Taking the pill was simple, but the feelings that came with it were not.

My father didn't look like the other dads, who went to work wearing suit jackets. He lived in his work clothes: T-shirts and jeans. He didn't work in an office—never did, never would—so he had no reason to dress other than exactly how he wanted. The definition of big and tall, his hands were often dirty and his farmer's tan a sign of mid-summer. And in place of the simple mustaches worn by other dads, my father's trademark feature was his long black beard. I've never seen my father's chin. When he's happy, his brown eyes twinkle, just like Laura Ingalls Wilder described her pa's eyes in the Little House books. Falling asleep at night, few things comforted me more than hearing his laughter echo through the house. He would make mental notes of our interests and surprise us with thoughtful trinkets.

He liked to take my siblings and me to the movies on days we didn't have to go to school. We would get a large-sized popcorn and sit in a single row, passing the giant bag back and forth while grabbing handfuls. If the movie was really good, we'd tell my nine-to-five working mom about it at dinner, reciting our favorite lines and laughing over the best parts.

Nothing ever, ever got past him. I could half-ass chores with my mother, but with him, no way.

"You didn't vacuum the whole floor. The whole floor includes under your bed," he'd say, looking underneath my twin bed.

"Dad," I'd whine, "it's close enough."

"It's not enough. Finish the job and you'll be done."

My father was also the oldest of his siblings. I got my tiny, upturned nose from him, and his personality, too. Stubborn, independent, and impatient, we share the horrible need to have the last word in every argument. My mother and sister, on the other hand, are both middle children. By birth-order destiny, they were able to tolerate our tempers, egos, and bossy attitudes. It's not surprising that I was my mother's child and my sister was Daddy's Girl.

Everything I know about my father, his family, and his childhood, I learned through my mother. She was the one who explained away his anger and his frustrations.

"Your dad wanted to be a veterinarian," the story went, "but when it came time to apply for colleges, his grades weren't good enough. So he had to go to trade school, and he doesn't want the same for you. He wants you to be able to do whatever you want."

My dad was away from home for half of the year, working on cargo ships, and the other half he spent playing Mr. Mom. He braided my sister's hair, made our lunches, and took me to my doctor's appointments while my mother worked as a nine-to-five nurse. He wanted a better life for me, and tough love was his means of motivation. I didn't know how to express, at the time, how suffocating his expectations could be. He never used the word "perfect," but that's how I felt he wanted me to be.

"If you ever get detention," he told me on the first day of fourth grade, "you're walking home."

We didn't live far from school, but this threat was the cruelest punishment I could imagine. It was the height of 1990s stranger danger. No one in my class walked to or from school. Everyone either rode the bus or got a ride from their parents. To make me stand out as the one kid who walked home made the potential punishment even worse.

I tried for months to be good, to do my homework, to get to class on time, to remember the right school supplies. I would get frustrated at myself for struggling to do the things that other kids seemed to do with ease, like staying in my seat and raising my hand before I spoke. One day, all my failures collided and I got my first detention slip.

I cried in front of the entire class when it happened. Everyone laughed at my overreaction, even my teacher, while I fizzed with embarrassment. But it wasn't detention or the humiliation of crying in front of the class that filled me with dread. It was the punishment that would follow my punishment.

Detention itself was uneventful. For one hour after school, I had to write, in my best cursive handwriting, five ways in which I would improve so I wouldn't receive those demerits again. My mind was on the walk home from school the entire time. I couldn't believe I had to walk alone. I wasn't even allowed to wait for the bus by myself, and yet he wanted me to do this. The world could take me! Then he'd be sorry. Then he'd miss me. Then he'd see that this was a huge mistake.

My heart lifted when I saw my father through the school's glass doors. He wasn't going to going to make me walk home after all! He'd come to school to pick me up.

Before I could say anything, he took the backpack from my back, opened the passenger seat, and put it inside. He shut the door again.

"All right," he said. "Start walking."

My mouth fell open.

"Dad. No."

He scowled and his voice got louder. "This is not a surprise, Andrea. I told you this was going to happen. Don't act like this."

I whined and pleaded for a few more minutes, but it was no use. He had zero sympathy.

The other detention attendees were now leaving school, walking to waiting cars and getting inside. It felt like everyone was watching us.

"Fine," I sputtered, and turned to walk in the direction of our house, the fringe on my denim cowgirl jean jacket fluttering with every step. I started to cry.

And I cried the entire way, my feelings a mixture of shame, anger, and self-pity. Big, fat, pitiful tears that ran down my cheeks and onto my Peter Pan collar. Why couldn't I have a normal dad who picked me up from detention like everyone else? Why was he so mean? Why did he hate me so much?

All the while, my father drove extremely slowly beside me, watching me. I never glanced over my shoulder, but I could hear the motor behind me. I walked past familiar sights, which looked different from this new perspective: the day care center I sometimes went to after school; Cameron Court, where I played basketball in the summer. I turned right from Prospect Street toward Pittsburgh Street, which took me past the library, two gray stone churches, and up the hill toward home.

"I hate him," I thought. "I hate him so much. He's the worst dad in the world, and he must hate me, too, to make me do this." My heart burned with resentment. I made up my mind: I had no choice but to run away at the first opportunity. Clearly, I could no longer live in that house. He obviously didn't care about me. I would be doing him a favor by leaving. I wasn't good enough for him and I never would be.

When we were half a block from home, our house within sight, he sped up, thinking he would meet me there.

"This is my chance," I thought.

I turned on my heel and sprinted in the opposite direction for two blocks before I stopped to catch my breath. The house next to me was missing a length of drainpipe, allowing water from an earlier rainfall to splash from the roof onto the ground. I put my head underneath the stream.

"This is how I'll take a shower on the streets," I thought. I was a nine-year-old in a Catholic school uniform, and I really, truly believed I would never go home again.

I heard a screech of tires from behind me, and I turned to see the family minivan roar up the street and pull to a stop right next to me. My eyes widened with shock. I was too frightened to move. He was looking for me?

"Get. In. The. Car." He spoke between clenched teeth.

Before I got in, I saw it. I didn't believe it at the time, because I thought fear was an emotion that disappeared well before adulthood. But I now know it for what it was. Past the anger, I saw his fear. He was afraid of losing me. Me, the imperfect mess.

At home, he screamed and lectured for hours, his anger filling the house.

"Why would you run away when you were so close to home?" he shouted. "It's not like you didn't know where to go, Andrea."

"I don't know!" I yelled back, over and over, too embarrassed to say that I'd wanted never to go home again. I was often expected to explain my impulsiveness, but my ability to articulate my tangled feelings got lost somewhere between my heart and my throat. I hurt all the time. Didn't they understand that?

A dozen detentions would add up, over those early years, for my typical indiscretions: tardiness, talking out, forgetfulness. Despite all that, and without discussion, I would never again walk home from detention.

The Happiest Days of Our Lives
Rebecca College

"**N**OT THIS TIME, BECKY," my father says without remorse, "I'm just too busy—have too much to do."

I hang up and spin on my heel to face my husband, seething.

"He's too fucking busy to see us. To see his grandkids! What the hell does he have to do on a Saturday afternoon? It's not like he's taking care of my mom anymore!"

My husband, Tim, comes over and squeezes my shoulder as if trying to open up a pressure valve, knowing I would push away a hug. He's long been a witness to the tension between my dad and me, but the tension seems to be frustratingly one-sided this time.

I shrug off his hand and pace, furious. "It would have been two hours, only two hours, to go with Mom and us to lunch. And his only grandchildren! Who he gets to see—what—once a month, if that? Nice that he fucking cares. What am I supposed to do with this? Seriously, what?"

Tim slowly shakes his head. "Nothing. He's not going to change. Try to let it go."

I take a deep breath and let it out slowly, trying to do just that: let it go. I don't want to allow my father's behavior to ruin another visit.

It will be our first chance to visit my mom, who has recently been placed in a "memory care" facility at an assisted living home. Her battle with dementia has been developing slowly for years, recognizably since I was a teenager, but it really all started while she was in Vietnam. In the past twelve months, it became harder and harder to ignore that she was more than "just forgetful." My father, her caregiver, had tried to deny or explain away her condition for years, but her problems came to a head two months ago, when she again had to be committed to a psychiatric ward for her depression and memory lapses. He could no longer look the other way, could no longer pretend she would be safe if he just kept her home.

I came home from high school to find her asleep on the couch. She was bundled up in her pale pink bathrobe, another day spent in her pajamas. She'd been "sick" for weeks, but regardless of the hours and days she spent resting, she appeared to be no closer to recovery.

"Becky, in the kitchen," my dad called out in an unusually calm voice. I dumped my book bag in the hallway and walked as far as the threshold of the kitchen, where I slouched in the doorway, unwilling to commit to sharing the room with him. From this spot I was able to participate in a conversation with my dad—seated at the round table, leaning on it with his forearms to support a portion of his formidable weight—while sneaking glances at my mom in the living room.

"What." It wouldn't do to give him the respect he felt he deserved.

"As I'm sure you've noticed, Mom isn't well. She's going to be going away for a while next week."

"Where?"

"She's severely depressed and has been having nightmares, flashbacks. Her PTSD . . . she'll be going to a VA hospital for a few months."

It wasn't as if this were the first time the VA was mentioned in our house; my parents had a long and complicated relationship with the

Department of Veterans Affairs. Both had gone through counseling at the VA in the early years of my life. The experience was my father's first—and last—attempt at therapy. His psychologist "betrayed him," an unforgivable sin that reinforced his view that the world was a horrible place where no one was worthy of trust. My mom went to both a psychologist and a support group for Vietnam Vets, specifically for women. As a kid I was dragged along, spending evenings in someone's office, playing make-believe with another vet's child, inventing worlds under desks and in cabinets while my mother found comfort in these women's shared experiences. I knew even then that the VA was a part of my parents' lives, that it always would be, and this knowledge was confirmed year after year as I grew older and began to understand that their health would always be tied to their statuses as "vets."

"How is sending her away going to help?" I snarled, as if I knew better. I began kicking the edge of the door trim with the toe of my Doc Marten, hoping I could channel my confusion and fear into that piece of paneling while hiding these feelings from my dad. As apathetically as I could, I croaked out, "Well, who's going to take care of me?"

He cleared his throat deeply and with clear agitation—yes, I'd scored a hit!—and answered sternly, "Me. Who do you think?"

I snorted and turned to leave, to escape to my bedroom, when he cleared his throat again to get my attention. I paused and turned my head as little as possible, implying that I was listening without having to look him in the eye.

"You just make it worse, you know. You're the reason she can't get better. You're the reason she has to go away."

My parents met in 1967, both stationed near Pleiku while serving in the United States Army. Men the country over were holding their breath in the hope that their numbers wouldn't be called for the draft, but despite this and the escalating violence in Vietnam, both my father and mother went voluntarily. My father, a delinquent from the streets of Queens, had hoped that enlisting would give him some control over where he was sent; my mother, a girl who had only left her native Bethlehem, Pennsylvania, twice before graduating from nursing school, wanted "to see the world, to have an adventure." Each was on active duty for only two years, but within that twenty-four-month span they would travel the world, meet each other, and be exposed to horrors they would never be able to process.

Post-traumatic stress disorder is not a new medical diagnosis. It has been known as a real and serious condition for decades, but only in the past five or ten years has it started to be acknowledged as the severely life-altering and potentially life-threatening disorder that it is, especially for the population that so often carries the diagnosis: combat veterans. Thousands of veterans had come home witnesses of the tragedies of guerrilla warfare only to be taunted and harassed. It was believed that once you were stateside, you should forget what you saw and get on with your life. Dwelling on the past wouldn't help, and if you were having trouble coping, maybe you just needed to "toughen up."

I don't know how soon my parents were diagnosed with PTSD after they returned to the US, or if they even believed it when they heard the words. Neither do I remember the age at which I first became aware of those four letters and the weight they carried within our home. But I knew from some of my earliest days that my parents had served not only in the military but in Vietnam, and that it continued to impact their actions, moods, and health. When I was five, I helped clean the Vietnam Memorial with members of Rolling Thunder; when I was seven, I watched *Good Morning, Vietnam* with my folks before I understood any of the references; when I was sixteen . . .

Once down the hall and in my bedroom, my ritual began: I shut my door as hard as I could without it being a "slam," turned on my stereo, and collapsed onto my mattress. The music was always aggressive and loud, but that day I wasn't listening. I was hunched over and sobbing, wracked with the guilt of what I feared I'd done to this woman I loved, while also barely able to suppress my rage at that man in my kitchen.

As my energy waned and my tears subsided, I was able to focus on the stereo, quieting for a moment before "Comfortably Numb" began to fill my bedroom. If only I could be, I thought.

When I was a little girl, my father, in his darkest moments, would lock himself away in the basement and blast music, although I would have been hard-pressed to call it such at the time. Through the floor I could hear the whir of helicopters, the squeal of guitars, the chanting of children—and his screams, primal and bloodcurdling.

"When your dad comes back upstairs, let's remember to stay out of his way. He may be a bit upset. This is a hard time for him," my mom would gently but firmly remind my brother and me, as if we needed such a suggestion. I wanted nothing to do with him. I wanted only to hide in my closet with my sock monkey and hope the screaming would stop. And when it did, when he emerged to be with his family, I wanted nothing more than to disappear, to be invisible, so that his screams wouldn't turn on me.

Years later, I would be able to identify the music of those daytime nightmares as Pink Floyd's *The Wall*, a concept album dealing with isolation and abandonment. When I finally discovered the record for myself, I found it oddly soothing, feeling that its main character somehow knew *me*, knew how *I* felt. It helped me through my darkest moments, trying as I was to live in a world created and controlled by two damaged people. Little did I realize, at the time, that the music that helped me to feel that I could survive another day had also kept my father going a decade before. We both found solace in these musical tales of isolation, but was I also finding a piece of my father? He'd felt *then* the way I felt *now*; was this the subconscious bridge I had been searching for?

—

My mom came home after two months in the PTSD unit of a VA Hospital; or rather, her shell did. The time had passed without incident at home, mainly because my father and I retreated into our own rooms and worlds, crossing paths only when absolutely necessary. ("Becky, here's a hundred dollars. I'm going to drop you off at the grocery store tomorrow morning and pick you up after an hour. We need milk.") Upon returning, she floated through the house, wandering from room to room, sitting for a minute or an hour and then moving on, staring at the walls as if they could provide her some answer. Our kitchen table became a landscape of little orange bottles. She had always taken a lot of medication—for arthritis, irritable bowel syndrome, a racing heart—but the collection more than doubled and now included antidepressants, anti-anxiety pills, and sleep aids. I stood in the doorway and watched her open and close each bottle, organizing the pastel tablets in groupings that seemed to make sense to her. As she closed yet another lid, she looked up and noticed me watching.

"Don't get old," she said with a smile that didn't reach her eyes. "It's the pits."

"You're not old," I wanted to shout, "you have so much life left, if you would just wake up!" She was only fifty-three, yet it seemed as if she could be eighty-three. Those two damn years just kept robbing her of more.

It would take her months, if not years, to get back to some approximation of herself. Her journey toward healing is another story in and of itself, a tale of beautiful moments bogged down by a heaviness deep within. She would continue to have spells, to feel "punky," as she taught us to call the blues, growing up. And she would have a few scares: an accidental overdose here, a forgetful moment there. My father, who had very deliberately refused to accept treatment for his own PTSD, continued to withdraw further into himself. He faced my mom's PTSD head-on every day, but somehow he could never address his own inner torment. Dad and I would continue to fight; my teenage angst wasn't quelled and my personal struggle with depression wasn't over, but in those two months alone together, we had forged a truce.

I grew up knowing that there were holes in my knowledge, that there were pieces of their stories that as a child I couldn't and shouldn't know. But I always thought I would sit down, once we were all in a better place, and hear their stories as an adult, when I could try to understand these two people and come to terms with the life I'd grown up in. But we never would be in that better place. Now, the story is slipping away along with my mom, and I find myself trying to grasp it ever harder.

It's a beautiful autumn day, and the sun shines through the windshield as we make our way down the small streets that take us to the facility.

"There," I say, pointing across the dashboard to a driveway marked by a wayfinding sign. We turn in and head toward a large building with long, white columns supporting a roof that covers the wraparound drive leading to the front door. After parking and unbuckling the kids, we shuffle our feet through the fallen leaves on the sidewalk.

"Crunch, crunch, crunch," my one-year-old son mimics. "Crunchy LEAVES!"

As we get closer to the door, I go over the facts with my daughter one more time. I try in all aspects to be as honest with my children as possible, and I feel that this is no different. But how do you explain to a four-year-old why Grammy doesn't live at home anymore? We've talked about Grammy being sick but not in a way you can see, and Tim and I have tried to impress upon her that this isn't necessarily something Grammy would want to talk about, but who knows what sinks in to that still-developing brain? Underestimating her

15

has only proved us foolish, so we keep feeding her facts, and today is no different.

"There will be lots of other people inside, and they may be sick. So please don't run, and stay close to us, and let's use our inside voices. But we'll walk around and see Grammy's room and where she hangs out and eats her meals, and maybe we'll meet some of her friends, okay?" I try to summarize.

"Okay, Mama, okay. I know. You already told me this."

We walk through the lobby, and I can't help but scan the place, trying to get a feel for the living conditions based on the furniture and environment. There's a middle-aged man and his son playing chess at a coffee table—just visitors, no doubt, but the fact that they seem so comfortably settled in gives me room to exhale the breath I wasn't aware I'd been holding. We head toward the elevators, the long hair of my babes swinging back and forth as they race to press the button. Once upstairs and at my mom's door, they knock and shout "Grammy!" and bounce with excitement. I hear her start to welcome us even before the door opens, and as she pulls it back, she is rushed by two squealing little beings, one hugging each leg. I can see their huge smiles as their faces smoosh into her, and the expression on her face mirrors their own—pure, innocent joy.

Tim reaches over and squeezes my hand. "She's okay," he whispers. "You?"

I nod and smile, blinking back a few stray tears. My past and my future stand before me, beautiful and radiant and happy. And at least on this day, being with them, I am too.

White Rabbit

Matthew Newton

"IT'S TERRIBLE HERE AT NIGHT," Sesha said. She was sitting across the table from me in the psychiatric ward at Forbes Regional Hospital, dressed in a T-shirt and sweatpants, her make-up washed away. We were alone in the day room, late November casting long rectangles of sunlight across the white tile floor. Behind us was a darkened television set, mounted on a metal support arm that reached out from the wall; puzzles and board games were stacked high on a nearby shelf.

It was Thanksgiving 1992. I was fifteen years old and in the tenth grade. Sesha was fourteen. Out in the hallway, prepackaged meals of turkey, stuffing, mashed potatoes, and cranberry sauce—all shrink-wrapped on plastic trays filed neatly in a stainless steel cart—were being delivered to patients. A male orderly in scrubs lumbered down the corridor, wheeling the cart from room to room, the unmistakable scent of hospital food strong in the air. Sesha still didn't have much of an appetite, so we sat and talked while the other patients ate quietly in their rooms.

"What do you mean by 'terrible'?" I asked, worried.

"That guy at the desk? Scott? He hits on all the girls here," she said. "But he waits until late at night. He's a pervert." Her ponytail had come loose, so she removed the elastic band that had held it in place, and for a moment her auburn-colored hair fell to her shoulders.

"He thinks he's attractive or something—it's weird," Sesha said, pulling her hair into a tight new ponytail.

"Has he hit on *you*?" I asked.

"Yes," she said, as if I were a fool for asking. "But don't worry. It's not like I'm going to sleep with him."

The thought hadn't even entered my mind. At least, not until she planted it there. It was a practice she had mastered in the three months since our first kiss: sowing seeds of doubt at any opportunity. But even though I was aware of the ways she often tried to manipulate a situation, the line between fantasy and reality remained impossibly hard to determine.

Sesha and I had been together only since late August, but we had known each other for more than a year. We met in ninth grade art class, a general curriculum course taught by a woman who was rumored to have been a Playboy centerfold in the 1960s. Sesha flirted with me from the first day of class, touching my arm when we talked and whispering to me between the teacher's lessons. We shared a similar sense of humor, dry and sarcastic, and easily fell in together. That she was smart and attractive only helped to magnify my self-consciousness each time we talked.

Sesha was from a multiracial family, part white and part Indian. Her dark, shoulder-length hair she often gathered and pulled to one side of her neck—usually the side opposite from where I sat—as she worked, exposing her full profile so I could see her lips and neckline, the curve of her jaw and the silver hoops in her pierced ears. She exuded a confidence I had never seen before, a confidence that would later evolve into a strange power over me.

I couldn't tell if Sesha was lying about Scott, a middle-aged man with dark, close-cropped hair and wire-rimmed glasses. His particular role on the ward was unclear, but he seemed to be an administrator, someone with a background in therapy, perhaps, who had taken on the role of staff manager. My only interactions with him were when I signed in at the front desk before each visit. He had been pleasant in our limited encounters. Was he capable of making sexual advances toward a teenage girl?

"Tell me what I should do," I said. "I can help." My mother, who was reading a book in the waiting room outside the ward, had been doing her best to advocate for Sesha; I figured if any of this were true, maybe she could help. What worried me, of course, was Sesha's tendency to exaggerate. Her desire to place herself at the center of the drama, whether real or imagined, was an aspect of her personality I'd never quite understood, especially considering that her life was chaotic enough on its own. Six days earlier, that chaos had pushed her into the psychiatric ward at Forbes—a move that turned out to be less the signal of an unsettled mind than a measure she took to establish a safe distance from her father.

"I can't go home tonight," Sesha had said. "He'll kill me." A strict Indian man, her father's temper and authority loomed like a monolith over her family's household. We were in my bedroom at my parents' house when she said this. It was the Friday before Thanksgiving, and Sesha had ridden home with me on the bus after school. Her deep brown eyes welled with tears as she talked, mascara running in inky-black dots against her olive cheeks. In her right hand was a copy of her report card. She had received two Ds for the semester: one in science, the other in gym. She cut each class regularly, often meeting me under a quiet stairwell we had found in one of the school's back hallways, where we would fool around or daydream about the future. Other times, it was to smoke pot on the hiking trail behind the school with some of the stoners she knew.

To Sesha's father, a report card with failing grades was unaccept-able. It didn't fit with his image of his daughter or the distinct ideas he had for her future. As she explained it, her father expected she would graduate at the top of her class, go on to a respected four-year university—somewhere like Case Western Reserve—and then consider her options for graduate school. The details got murkier after that, but there was often talk, however serious or not, of an arranged marriage with a young man from another Indian family. It was a daunting vision. But the fact that her father had no idea of what was actually going on in her life—and what he might do if he found out—seemed to scare her the most.

"I don't know how to explain this to him," Sesha said, holding up her report card. Her voice was fragile, breaking apart a little at the end of each word. She was sitting on the blue carpet in my bedroom, her knees tucked tight to her chest, her back against the closet door. A miniature Chicago Bulls basketball hoop, a gift from my parents when I was in junior high, hung several feet above her head at the top of the door.

It was strange to see Sesha so upset. The only times she ever showed signs of fear were when her father came up in conversation. Though he worked long hours as a nuclear physicist at a nearby re-search facility, his presence in her life was constant and pervasive. Pleasing him was not necessarily something she wanted to do, but it was an obligation that colored many of her decisions. Given his own accomplished career, Sesha's father expected academic excel-lence from each of his four children—three daughters and a son— and his discipline often turned physical when he was disappointed with them.

A year earlier, before we were dating but when we nevertheless spent hours on the phone after school each day, Sesha had told me that her father once pushed Abeer, her younger brother, down a flight of stairs. The fall was violent and left her brother, who was in grade school at the time, with a broken arm. Sesha couldn't remember what it was that had set her father off, but that was the point. His reactions were as unpredictable as his temper.

Since I had never met or even seen Sesha's father, except in photographs, a certain kind of mystery surrounded him. The framed pictures in her house revealed a short, dark-skinned man with tinted glasses and a crown of thinning black hair. It was intentional, of course, that we had never met. He forbade any of his three daughters from having a boyfriend. Sesha's mother, however, a timid but pleasant American woman, was far more lenient. Unlike her husband, she was well aware that each of her three daughters secretly had boyfriends. When I would visit Sesha after school, her mother was particularly nice to me. She would make us food and tell bad jokes as we sat around the kitchen table. I would help her carry groceries from the trunk of her Pontiac LeMans, or play video games with Abeer. It all felt extremely normal. But there was always the knowledge that the fun was temporary, a welcome but finite lull before Sesha's father returned home.

"I'm afraid what I might do if I go home tonight," Sesha said, wiping away tears as she looked up at me from the bedroom floor, her eyes searching, it seemed, for some sort of reaction.

"What's that mean?" I asked, hearing a familiar tone of frustration in my voice. I wanted Sesha to be clear about what it was she was hinting at, to just come out and say it.

"You really don't know?" she asked, sounding irritated. "Never mind then."

I knew she was threatening suicide, or at least some type of harm to herself, if she had to go home and face her father. But I also questioned how serious she was, knowing the pleasure she took in helping a situation unravel. The last thing I wanted was to further agitate her. But I also didn't want to play along. I had done so in the past. Not with threats of suicide, but with other issues just as serious.

Earlier that year, Sesha had told me that a varsity soccer player had raped her at a party when she was a freshman. Her account of what the boy had done was matter-of-fact, almost emotionless, and caught me by surprise. Learning that someone had done this to her drove me into a rage. The next day I confronted the boy in a hallway at school, asking him bluntly what had happened at that party. A fight broke out. Teachers quickly intervened and separated us, and as they dragged us to the principal's office, the boy laughed at me for believing Sesha's story, telling me I was too gullible. At the time, I ignored him. I was in the right, I assumed, because why would Sesha lie about such an awful experience? But as the months wore on, I began to question her stories and her reasons for telling them. Our relationship had proven that I was one of the few people Sesha trusted—her confidence in me often revealed in quiet, intimate moments—but that didn't deter her from lying to me when it was convenient. So many of our conversations were like falling down a rabbit hole, the truth so obscured it seemed impossible to set any of it right in my head.

I sat on the floor next to Sesha and held her hand. The house was warm, but her fingers felt cold.

"You don't know him," she said about her father, her voice soft again. She reminded me that it was impossible for me to know how he would react. She was right.

Out in the kitchen, my grandmother was checking on a pot roast she had put in the oven several hours earlier. The smells of seasoned meat and roasted potatoes reminded me of when she used to cook for my sister and me when we were little, before I had problems that couldn't be solved.

I looked at Sesha. Her eyes were red, the skin above and below her lashes tender at the edges, but she wasn't crying anymore. Before I could say anything, she interrupted.

"I'm not going home," she said. "I'll kill myself if I do."

"It's probably just playful flirting," Sesha said when I pressed her about Scott. "You shouldn't worry." We were walking laps around the outer edges of the ward, watching the clock as 8 p.m. approached and visiting hours came to a close.

"You would tell me if you needed me to do something, right?" I asked as we stopped outside her hospital room.

"I'm fine," she said, softening a bit. "It's okay here."

We said goodbye for the night. I kissed her and we hugged for what felt like several minutes. After all she'd told me since I arrived, I was afraid to leave. But I couldn't stay any longer, either. "Visiting hours are over for the evening," a voice boomed from the small circular speakers in the ceiling. "Please remember to sign out at the front desk and wait for a staff member to buzz you out."

I signed the log, scrawling my signature next to the date and time of my visit. On my way out of the ward I looked over my shoulder and saw Scott standing there motionless, his eyes fixed on the exit.

Out in the waiting room I found my mother sitting on a couch near a bank of vending machines. The other chairs and small couches were all empty; rows of fluorescent tube lights hummed loudly overhead. She looked tired but smiled when she saw me.

"How is she?" my mother asked, tucking the paperback she had been reading into her purse.

"Okay, I guess," I said, rubbing my eyes, which felt heavy and dry. It was hard to hide how tired I felt. My mother's face fell a little when she noticed, a look of pity more than anything else. The last few days had been like trying to sleep through a fever. I felt uncomfortable when I was with Sesha and out of place with my parents, as if I were living in an alternate reality. I wanted to hug my mother but I didn't. The space between us felt too heavy.

"She's in a better mood than yesterday," I added, keeping Sesha's story about Scott to myself. "Still not eating much though."

"Hospital food is the pits," she said, smiling a bit. "Don't worry, she's gonna bounce back."

I was grateful for my mother's support, but I could tell it was a struggle for her to stay positive. Besides my relationship with Sesha, the last year had been difficult for our family. Since my freshman year, my mood and state of mind had started to shift. I spent more time by myself; I slept long hours and was impossible to wake in the mornings; and I was regularly acting out of character, reacting with fits of anger and nearly constant irritability to everyone around me. But the most dramatic change was a number of compulsive and increasingly odd behaviors: constantly checking door locks, washing my hands excessively, and counting every footstep. I developed an irrational and overwhelming concern that any word I spoke would offend someone. It was maddening.

My erratic behavior and the severity of my new habits had my parents concerned. So, after months of resisting, I finally agreed to an evaluation at Western Psychiatric Institute and Clinic (WPIC). Sesha was committed to the psych ward at Forbes just two weeks before my evaluation, when I would be formally diagnosed with severe clinical depression and obsessive-compulsive disorder. It proved that my parents' fears were not unfounded. Something *was* wrong with me.

"This is more than you can fix," my mother said, referring to Sesha and her problems with her father. "The best you can do is to be there for her, be a good listener."

It was Thanksgiving night. We were seated at the lunch counter in a Denny's, set amidst the suburban sprawl near the hospital, finishing our dinners. On my mother's plate was a hot turkey sandwich, half eaten and the gravy now cold. Crumbs from a BLT dotted my plate, the inedible crusts discarded in a tidy semicircle. Our receipt, which the waitress had set down in a wet ring left by my water glass, lay on the counter. I picked up the soggy piece of paper and handed it to my mother, who looked at my hands, dry and irritated from too much washing.

"Dad can take you to the hospital tomorrow, if you want," she said as we stood up and walked to the cash register. She rifled through her purse as she talked, searching for her wallet.

I wondered what version of Sesha I might see the next day. Would she be rational and kind, like she'd been in the final minutes before we said goodbye? Or would she be spiteful, talking in half-truths that left my brain in knots?

I would learn much later that my parents, particularly my mother, had deep concerns about Sesha's influence on me. In the notes from my initial evaluation at WPIC, the clinician wrote: "Matt's mother reports that he may speak to his girlfriend on the phone 6–7 times per night, and she is concerned that he feels responsible for her psychological well-being. Mrs. Newton also stated the concern that somehow Matt's girlfriend would push him into a joint suicide."

My mother smiled as she handed the bill and her credit card to the man behind the cash register.

"Was everything okay tonight?" he asked, a pleasant look on his face.

"Yes," my mother said. "Everything was fine."

Staying

Tahirah Alexander Green

ON FRIDAY, FEBRUARY 25, 2011, a nineteen-year-old college soph-omore lost her shit. She was usually a responsible person. Too responsible, even. The kind of person who made a plan for how to plan. As a freshman, she'd created a detailed chart of requirements and course options for her next three years at university. Her preparation wasn't completely absurd: She was the type of person who tripped up stairs and forgot what it was that she'd forgotten.

On the day she lost her shit, her body, which swung like a pendulum from a size eight to a size twelve, was in mid-swing at ten and a half. This meant that none of her pants fit properly. As a logical response to this, she wished she had a bigger ass. She also wished that her chemically relaxed hair would grow long and healthy. Instead, it was breaking off for the third time since she was thirteen, leaving a frizzy, chin-length mess sprouting from her scalp.

It was winter, so her brown skin was running high yellow, mean-ing it was getting closer to the "light, bright, and nearly white" side of blackness. She preferred her skin to be darker because she associated the tone with summer. She preferred summer. The gray skies and cold temperatures of winter debilitated her.

Nearsighted, she wore sienna wire-framed glasses that she lost regularly, as she lost most of her things. Her cell phone, her identification card, her planner. It was a tendency she counteracted with early preparation for everything, an attempt to give herself enough time to find whatever item she would inevitably misplace along the way. As a backup strategy, she would tell her friends where she put things so they could remind her later.

That Friday night, though, she lost something intangible. She tried to understand it, explaining the loss through lengthy text messages to one of her best friends. Variations of the sentence "I don't want to feel anymore" transformed into "I don't want to live anymore." Her friend had heard these sentiments before, but tonight was different. Tonight the messages came rapidly, with vivid descriptions of the kinds of harm she'd like to do to herself. Her friend tried to calm her down, even rushing over to her dorm room late at night to watch over her. Her friend tried to remain calm as she explained to the 911 operator that something was wrong with Tahirah.

"Wouldn't you like to take a leave of absence?" Shernell, the student affairs representative, asked, hands folded in her lap. She was a plump black woman in her thirties, with a hair tie stretched thin over the long braids that hung past her shoulders. She stared across a small, round table in her dimly lit office at Tahirah, whom she called variations of *Tah-har-ah* no matter how many times she was informed that the correct pronunciation was *Ta-here-rah*.

Tahirah shook her head and prepared the words in her mind before speaking. She was terrified of being inarticulate. Being inarticulate led to nights of insomnia, the poorly chosen words playing on repeat in her mind. Sometimes she thought of better, more precise words and berated herself for not having said them.

"No," Tahirah answered. "It's easier to stay here."

Shernell looked at her, incredulous. Tahirah understood her confusion. Two weeks ago, on her way back from the dorm's laundry room with the friend who had called 911, Tahirah had stepped out of an elevator to see two campus police officers loitering outside her door. She walked past them into the small, cluttered square that was her dorm room. The wood floor was covered with shredded yarn from a crochet project she'd abandoned a few hours ago, when distraction had stopped serving as a suitable coping method. Shreds of white paper also covered the floor; she'd chosen to slice them instead of her skin. Jewelry, crochet patterns, coins, medication, half-empty Gatorade bottles, and tissues upon tissues were strewn across her desk.

"So, how's it going?" one of the officers, the younger of the pair, asked her. His hands were in his pockets and he seemed optimistic, even cheerful.

She shrugged.

"Is everything okay?"

She avoided eye contact, said "Mmhmm."

"So what's going on over here? Want to explain this?" the older officer asked curtly. He stood with his arms akimbo, nodding his head towards a neon-orange knife skewered into a paper towel roll.

She shrugged.

"So . . . umm . . . you draw those?" the younger officer asked, gesturing to the *chibi* illustrations on her closet door.

"My brother did," she answered, her voice whispery and low.

"Oh, cool. What do your parents do?"

"My dad works at an airport."

The officer continued to attempt small talk while Tahirah stared at the floor. She hoped they wouldn't start searching the room. Her roommate would hate that. She'd already be pissed by how much of a mess Tahirah had made.

His attempt at small talk failing, the officer sighed. "We're not really trained to do this. I'm sorry."

Tahirah shrugged.

"We're going to take you to Western Psych's ER," said the older officer. "If you don't go voluntarily, we'll have to make you. Then they'll have to keep you for a while."

She shrugged. "Okay."

"Okay?" the older officer asked.

"I'll go."

When she arrived at Western Psychiatric Institute and Clinic, she passed through the metal detector, and security took her cell phone away. The rest of the night was spent doing paperwork and waiting to be seen by a doctor. The obnoxious laugh track of a '90s sitcom played intermittently from a television in the corner of the room. As time passed, she became increasingly uncomfortable. Hospitals were creepy, smelling like death and bleach.

Eventually she was summoned for her assessment. She did not make eye contact with the doctor, a white male whose face she wouldn't remember. The doctor asked her a series of questions she'd already been asked. Why was she here? How did she get here? She was sure that someone had already told him her earlier replies. She answered as concisely as possible.

"Are you taking medication?" he asked.

"No. Not now," she mumbled.

"Why not?"

If she'd been honest, she would've told him it was because she resented needing a little pill to function "normally." That even though she worked two part-time jobs, she was still pretty broke and couldn't always afford the Celexa. Her father's insurance was inconsistent with its coverage, and her family wasn't financially stable enough even to ensure shelter, let alone healthcare. She didn't want to talk about money, though; if she did, she might cry. Any sign of weakness might give them an excuse to keep her there.

"I was feeling better," she lied.

She'd read somewhere that it was common for individuals with mental disorders to discontinue their medications when their symptoms improved. She figured it would make her incident more justifiable. It'd be an easy fix: all she needed was to be drugged again.

"What triggered you tonight?" he asked.

Maybe it was residual disappointment from having to return home for winter break. Tahirah had been accepted into a program to build a library in Ghana, but in the end she couldn't afford to go. Instead, she got to remember that the past summer's foreclosure on her parents' home had actually happened, forcing her parents and siblings into a cramped apartment. Now she got to see her mother throwing tantrums, peeing herself and sobbing. Nothing about her mother resembled the woman she was before her stroke two years ago.

Maybe it was the guilt of escaping when her family couldn't. Maybe it was because of the Shittsburgh Gray—the persistent, sunless sky that Pittsburgh endures for months.

"I don't know," she answered.

The doctor explained that he thought it was because she'd gone off her meds. He let her leave.

Shernell drove Tahirah from the emergency room back to her dorm at four in the morning. Shernell was chosen for this task, Tahirah assumed, because she was the housefellow for her dormitory, Morewood Gardens. The housefellows were full-time staff members who were supposed to enrich the living experiences of residents in campus housing. They usually functioned behind the scenes, except when they provided free food, spammed students with emails, and in Shernell's case, served as amenable transport.

That night, Shernell convinced Tahirah to take a week off to regroup. Tahirah was hesitant to take her advice. She had already been sick with the flu and missed some classes, and her coursework remained one of the few things that hadn't slipped entirely out of her control. She didn't want to fuck that up. But Shernell seemed so calm, so confident. It'll be *fine*, Shernell assured her.

Before the week ended, Shernell would call to inform Tahirah that she was failing three classes. She hadn't failed a single assignment she'd completed prior to the call.

Before her trip to Western Psych, Tahirah had thought the spring semester was going well. She finally felt comfortable opening up to her psychiatrist, Dr. H, which meant that their sessions were no longer awkward silences during which Tahirah memorized the pattern of the office's carpet. Eight months of happy pills, an antidepressant called Celexa, seemed to be paying off.

She was working two campus jobs, which meant she rarely had to go through the guilt of asking her father for money he didn't have to spare. She could afford to buy some of her textbooks, for once, although she still acquired the majority through libraries and copyright-violating photocopies. More important, she was able to buy food and no longer had to mooch off her friends as she'd done the previous semester. Back home, food wasn't always guaranteed.

She shared a room with Michelle, an industrial design major who had also been her suitemate during freshman year. Their room was small, with every piece of furniture crammed next to the other and leaving only a small space in the center of the room. She'd previously lived in her grandmother's house—her mother's mother. This meant that when she cried, she was asked, "Why are you doing this to yourself?" Living with grandma meant she was supposed to suck it up and go to church. That, of course, was preferable to living with her parents.

Her parents and siblings—Taylor, twelve, and Jamal, seventeen— had recently moved into a two bedroom apartment after their home was foreclosed upon. Stuff that the household of five had accumulated over the years was piled into the narrow apartment. Her siblings each got their own room, while her parents shared a sectional sofa in the living room. Her cramped dorm room was certainly more spacious than her family's new home.

Her crowded room was where she spent the majority of her time, which was split between self-loathing and studying. She was enrolled in six academic courses and one student-taught course. This was considered an overload. She overloaded that semester, as she would every semester after her freshman year. This wasn't considered over-achievement at her university; this was common practice, and it suited Tahirah just fine. She preferred to keep busy. It kept her mind off of things at home.

She'd believed she was doing fine, academically. She'd missed a few days when she caught the flu, but had otherwise done far better, attendance-wise, than in any other semester. Yet here she was, mid-semester, with three of her professors claiming she was failing. Failing so badly, in fact, that they thought it wise for her to withdraw from their classes. It was an option she resisted not only because it would delay her graduation, but also because it would relegate her to part-time status, thereby risking the loss of her financial aid and housing.

These are the things Tahirah thought about as she tried to explain to Shernell why she didn't want to take a leave of absence. She didn't know how to properly articulate that she was choosing between a bad option and a worse one.

After it became clear to Shernell that Tahirah wouldn't be leaving, the list of individuals involved grew considerably. Discussions and emails culminated in a meeting with Tahirah, two professors, and the dean of her college.

She entered the Academic Advisory Center and sat awkwardly on a couch next to the two professors. One of them happened to be her academic advisor for creative writing, a thin woman with short and wavy brown hair. Her advisor was composed, as always, and today she seemed a bit cold, especially in comparison with the other professor. The other woman was chubby, with a loud voice, stringy reddish-brown hair, and thinning eyebrows that made her look perpetually annoyed.

Together they waited for the dean, who, Tahirah had been informed, would advocate on her behalf. Eventually the dean, a slim,
bespeckled woman with round glasses and hair cropped close to her
scalp, greeted them. She led them into a meeting room, where Tahirah sat beside her and across the table from her professors. The
meeting, which Tahirah had thought was intended to reach a com-
promise, soon became a rather one-sided discussion of the reasons
she would not be able to keep attending her classes. The professors
presented a united front, both steadfastly assured that Tahirah's
withdrawal from their courses was the best option—for them, at
least.

"The withdrawals from the classes won't be listed on your tran-
script. We'll erase them completely," the dean explained, a laugh in
her voice.

Tahirah wasn't sure why this was presented as if it were a favor;
the withdrawal deadline hadn't even passed yet. Her mind filled
with questions, making it difficult for her to prepare her words.
Why were the professors in the creative writing program unwilling to work with her? Her professors in the international relations
and politics program had agreed to let her make up the work she'd
missed during her regrouping period. They had even agreed to give
her extensions on her assignments, should she have an episode that
would impact her ability to complete them.

"The creative writing program is structured differently. Class par-
ticipation is more important," the professors each explained. So it
didn't matter that she completed her assignments; if she was too
depressed and anxious to be vocal, she was doomed. It was a line of
reasoning that would've been easier to accept if she hadn't taken a
screenwriting class the previous semester and silently earned an A.

"Your attendance hasn't been good," a professor added. While it
was true the she had missed classes because of the flu, those absenc-
es that had already been excused with a note from health services.
It was the time she'd taken off for her mental health that was inex-

cusable. Apparently, taking off that week to regroup hadn't been as okay as Shernell had believed it would be.

"The quality of your work has gone down," her advisor added.

So the checks and check pluses she'd received on her assignments —a maddeningly vague grading scale used in the creative writing program—had actually denoted failure.

"I can't even tell if you're doing the work," the other professor complained.

When she said that, Tahirah started to cry. She had stayed up late on so many nights to read and complete exercises for her classes, even during her "break." So much for control. This was what her illness meant: failure. It didn't matter that she was taking medication and seeing a therapist. The fact that she still panicked when she had to speak in front of a group meant she would never succeed. Soon she was crying because she was crying. She knew she was making a great case for herself, teary eyed and inarticulate.

"Okay," she said. She had to get out of the room.

The meeting being the epic failure that it was, Tahirah refused to let the semester end similarly. She added a mini-course to her schedule, giving her enough credits to still be considered a full-time student and keeping her financial aid in order. She researched the university's policy on financial aid for summer courses and convinced her advisor in international relations and politics to approve her taking classes at a university near home. This kept her graduation plans on track. She ended that semester with a solid GPA.

Her mental health remained far from stable. She feigned stability as best she could, so as not to arouse concern from professors and administrators, but in fact she'd grown more ashamed and despondent. She spent the majority of her free time sleeping, unconsciousness often being the only way she could bear to be around herself. She didn't socialize. The friend who had called 911 worried that Tahirah resented her and kept her distance. Michelle, her dorm mate, was kept frustratingly unaware of all that had happened. Tahirah had been too scared to tell her; what if Michelle would want to get rid of her too? And she shared with her family as little information as possible. They had enough to worry about.

Dr. H was beyond irritated; to her, Tahirah had been "punished for depression." Tahirah disagreed: it was her own fault. It was her own fault she was sick and her own fault she wasn't getting better. It would take a long time, but eventually she'd recognize that her illnesses weren't the problem. Those could be managed. But the stigma that came with them—the discomfort that mental illness evoked in others and the complex measures that people took to distance themselves from those feelings—was beyond her control. This was the real problem.

My Mantra

Linda K. Schmitmeyer

"**P**ASS THE KETCHUP," SAYS LUKE, already reaching across the dinner table to grab the Valu Time bottle from his big brother, John. I buy generic ketchup now, economy size, although there was a time when only Heinz graced our table.

It is a Friday evening in the spring of 1997, and our family is eating hamburgers and French fries. I didn't bother with a salad—too much effort at the end of a workweek. I'm at one end of our small kitchen table, purchased at a farm auction in Ohio shortly after Steve and I were married. We brought it with us when we moved to Pennsylvania a decade ago, along with other hand-me-down furniture and a barn full of antique farm equipment. Steve had accepted a job with SAE International, an engineering society headquartered about thirty minutes north of Pittsburgh. The move wasn't easy—it meant transporting several of Steve's full-size farm tractors, a goat, a pet rooster, a pair of geese, a barn cat and her kittens, and our dog, Otto—but Steve and I were excited about what lay ahead.

Seated opposite me is my husband of twenty-two years, whose gray, impassive eyes track the ketchup bottle as it moves back and forth across the table. Thirteen-year-old Luke sits to my right; John, seventeen, and my daughter Elly, seven, are on my left. Keeping Luke and Elly apart makes for more harmonious family meals, a tradition I cling to despite our challenges and even if we're only eating hamburgers and fries. I know Steve wants the ketchup but won't ask someone to pass it. Instead, he'll wait for the kids to finish and then reach across the table for it. Steve has changed in many ways since the onset of his mental illness several years ago. He's emotionally erratic and more combative when the mania flares, typical of someone with bipolar disorder. But he's also less confident in his interactions with others, hesitating to insert himself into any conversation. Never would I have imagined that this once-gregarious man would feel such uncertainty that he'd find it difficult to ask someone to pass the ketchup.

If I were feeling kinder, I'd enforce the traditional parenting roles in which I was raised. "Pass your father the ketchup," I'd say, suggesting that a parent should be served first. But not tonight. I feel vulnerable, worn out, and unsure of how much more I can take of living with a man who depends on me for everything, from following his medication regime to knowing what day it is.

I've been seeing a counselor off and on for several years now. Mostly we talk about coping with the multitude of changes brought about by Steve's illness: its effects on the children, the challenges of living with less money, my feelings of loss. At a recent visit, she asked me what I wanted from my relationship with Steve, and although I'd once told her that my life would be easier without him, I'd stopped short of saying I wanted out of the marriage. This time I answered, "I could never leave someone who's sick."

But that's not what she asked, I thought to myself. "You wouldn't leave somebody because they have cancer," I added, trying again.

Staying with Steve is tremendously difficult. For years now, I've been walking on eggshells around him, holding the family together while hoping the doctors will find medications to quiet his mind. I'm also always trying to accommodate him, giving in because I'm afraid he'll have another "episode" and disappear for a day or two without telling anyone where he's going. Leaving Steve feels impossible because he's trying to get better, but I wonder how much longer I can endure such an emotionally lopsided relationship.

As I rub my fingers along the kitchen table's chipped Formica top, I am reminded of my mother, who when faced with the many challenges of caring for her family frequently paraphrased a line from her favorite Robert Burns poem: "The best laid plans of mice and men go oft awry." Steve and I had planned to replace this table and some of the furniture we brought with us once he was established in his job. But that never happened.

I often think of my mother as I struggle to care for Steve and the children, especially now that there is less money than there used to be. She and my father, a baker, were ingenious when it came to providing for their large brood on his small salary. I'm the older of two girls in a family with ten boys. To make ends meet, Mother would sew our clothes and preserve hundreds of quarts of fruits and vegetables each summer, while my dad would mend our shoes and make laundry soap from lye and the bacon grease he brought home from the restaurant where he worked. Our lives were simple. I grew up in the 1950s in the small manufacturing town of Sidney, Ohio, and except for Sunday afternoon visits to relatives, our family traveled little. I was eleven years old the first time I left Ohio, and that was to see an aunt and uncle who'd moved to Indianapolis.

After high school, though, I wanted something more. I'd started talking about going away to college, which my father thought unnecessary. Early in my senior year when I was upstairs doing homework in my bedroom, a small pink-and-white room I shared with my sister, he appeared in the doorway. He'd just gotten home from the restaurant, and I knew something was up. He rarely initiated discussions with his children, preferring instead to leave the stickier issues of childrearing to Mother. "Why do you want to go to college?" he asked. To my father, who had grown up during the Depression and quit school after the eighth grade, a high school diploma was sufficient for a girl who was likely to marry her high school sweetheart. I didn't have a clear-cut plan for what I wanted to do after high school, but I knew I wanted a life grander than the one I was living. Going away to school seemed like a way to make that happen.

I met Steve at the University of Dayton, a small Catholic college forty miles south of my hometown. He'd grown up on a dairy farm not far from Sidney and was studying mechanical engineering. We started dating in our senior year and married several years later. After graduation, he worked as an engineer at Wright-Patterson Air Force Base in Dayton, and I taught English at a nearby high school. A dozen years and two children later, Steve accepted the job at SAE. We were both excited about the move, the beginning of what I thought would be an exciting new chapter in our life together.

Less than three years after our big move to Pennsylvania, I learned while sitting at this table that Steve had quit his job at SAE. He hadn't talked to me about leaving and didn't have another job lined up. By then we had three children, and although I taught writing two evenings a week at a local community college, I was mostly a stay-at-home mom.

I'd heard Steve's car pull into the driveway earlier than normal, which wasn't unusual when he had to travel the next day. He oversaw committees of engineers who developed standards for the aerospace industry, and he traveled frequently in the spring and fall of the year. Sometimes I went with him. The year before Elly was born, we traveled to Moscow for a meeting—far grander than my trip to Indianapolis so many years ago. When he was going to be away for several days, he often tried to get home to be with the boys when they got off the school bus.

I was sitting with all three kids at the table, talking to the boys as they ate their after-school snacks. John was in fourth grade, Luke in kindergarten; Elly would turn one later that month. As I looked out the window, I saw Steve crossing the cement slab at the end of our driveway, which he and his father had poured shortly after we moved.

At forty, Steve was still handsome, slender, and fit, with only hints of gray in his sandy blond hair. From afar, he looked like a successful businessman in a dark suit, his tie with red stripes loose around his neck. I liked to tease him by saying that up close he still looked like a farm boy, with his big hands and easy smile. That day, though, I could see that his face was drawn. He looked tired and nervous, a rarity for this confident, highly energetic man. And when he walked into the kitchen, without preamble and while the kids munched on pretzels and carrot sticks, he told me he'd quit his job.

Later, out of earshot of the children, he explained what had happened.

He'd been talking to his boss, Glenn, who'd recently joined SAE. Steve didn't particularly like working with him. They were discussing the new aerospace conference Steve was organizing at Wright-Patterson AFB, which he'd been asked to oversee because of his connections there. Planning a conference was less technical and more bureaucratic than Steve liked, and he often referred to the assignment as "glorified party planning."

According to Steve, they were discussing an issue about the conference—nothing out of the ordinary, just another thing they didn't agree on—when Glenn paused in the middle of the conversation. Then, as if wondering aloud, he asked Steve whether he thought SAE was a good fit for him. His tone was friendly, Steve said, "as if he knew I preferred engineering standards over organizing a conference. He didn't sound like someone who wanted to fire me."

The conversation continued, but Steve could see that something was on Glenn's mind. Never one to dance around a conversation, he confronted his boss point blank: "Glenn, do you think I should leave SAE?"

Glenn's lower lip quivered, Steve said, but he said nothing.

"I told him, 'Fine,' and slapped his desk. 'I'm out of here.' And I went right to Judy," who worked in Human Resources, "and told her I was quitting."

Steve soon found an engineering sales job in a small machine shop, only to be laid off six months later; this was followed by another sales job that lasted only four months. Then a college friend set him up as a technical sales rep for the plastics industry, and he started working from an office in our home. But sales were slow and our money stretched thin. I'd found full-time work at a weekly newspaper shortly after Steve left SAE, but my salary fell far short of what he'd made as an engineer. To get by, we sold the tractors and farm equipment he'd hauled from Ohio.

Around this time, Steve's mood began to change. The high spirits and animation that marked his early years were replaced by lows I'd not seen in our twenty years together. I would come home from work and frequently find him lying on our bedroom floor instead of working in his office. Steve had acquired the habit of relaxing on a floor from his father, who between farm chores would lie on the living room carpet because his work clothes were too dirty for the couch. When I'd urge him to work harder in his sales job, telling him that we needed his income to pay the bills, he'd complain that he didn't have the energy for work anymore.

"I just don't have the interest," he'd say, his words angering and confusing me. Sometimes I would call him lazy, and a fight would ensue. Other times I tried reasoning with him.

"Do you think I *want* to work all the time?" I'd say, and without waiting for answer, add, "I do it because I have to. I do it because my family needs me."

I often thought of his listlessness as a "mid-life crisis," figuring he was tired of our life together and wanted out of the marriage. He protested, saying he still loved me, yet fell deeper into lethargy. When I urged him to see a psychiatrist, he agreed, and she diagnosed him with "situational depression" and prescribed Prozac.

Although the antidepressant temporarily lifted his spirits, Steve continued to have trouble focusing on his engineering sales job. He began talking more about his concern with SAE's vice president, who was in charge of the society's day-to-day operations. Under his leadership, Steve said, the nonprofit neglected engineers working in their fields and focused too much on fundraising for SAE's Foundation, which had been established recently to support math and science education in high schools. He felt that the society needed a change in leadership and spearheaded an effort to make that happen. Although he hadn't worked there in several years, he was still a member of the Pittsburgh-area chapter and attended monthly meetings, where he talked to anyone who'd listen about his campaign against the VP. He also began spending more time at SAE headquarters' library, gathering information on the society's mission and obtaining the addresses of the board of directors, the members of which he planned to write with his concerns.

This was the early 1990s, and not even his psychiatrist thought of Steve's obsession with his former employer as mania. For many years, Steve had been a champion for SAE and its mission. He became a member of the student chapter in college, and when he worked at Wright-Patterson, membership in the Dayton chapter soared, due mostly to Steve's promotion of it. His efforts were recognized nationally when he was named one of the society's three Outstanding Young Engineers the year before he was hired as an SAE staff engineer. To me, though, his campaign against the vice president was just a diversion from his floundering sales job, and we argued bitterly.

"Why are you so worried about SAE now?" I wanted to know. "You left three years ago. Give it up!"

When he'd ignore my plea, I'd continue, "You spend so much time trying to fix an organization that doesn't care about you anymore. What about helping a family that needs you? I can't do this alone."

If I persisted in my efforts, he'd often say, "Somebody's got to stand up for what's right," a phrase I heard regularly as he became more and more engulfed by the mania.

Eventually, Steve's fixation caused us to separate, at least temporarily. Two months after moving out, he attended an SAE convention in Detroit with the hope of being able to address the board of directors about his concerns with the vice president's leadership. Although he didn't get to address the board, he did meet with its president, who told him to give up the cause and go home. With the convention drawing to a close and the window of opportunity to "fix" his beloved society narrowing, Steve went on a rampage through the convention center until the police arrived and hauled him away in handcuffs. He was hospitalized for a month, and his diagnosis of situational depression was changed to manic depression, or bipolar disorder as it's called today.

Three years later, after a mood stabilizer failed to quiet his obsessive thoughts about the engineering society, Steve's diagnosis was changed to schizoaffective disorder, which has some of the symptoms of schizophrenia but also the mood swings associated with bipolar disorder.

"Is there no end to this?" I asked my therapist after I told her of the change. We were talking about how doctors, lacking reliable biological markers that would signal a mental illness, rely mostly on a patient's behaviors when diagnosing a mental condition. I remembered Steve's abrupt departure from SAE, seven years earlier. It was the first symptom of his mental instability, although no one thought of it that way at the time.

Coming to grips with a severe mental illness takes a long time. Oddly, the breakdown in Detroit helped. Putting a label on Steve's campaign against the vice president was the first step in helping me to understand that he'd changed as a result of a medical condition, not because he didn't love me anymore.

But it's still hard for me to accept that people can't simply control their thoughts and actions; the idea runs contrary to the deeply seated notions of my youth, when my parents showed through their lives how one could overcome most challenges by merely setting one's mind to the task. What I didn't know then, though, was that you can't always rely on your mind to meet those challenges. Once energetic and determined, Steve can no longer trust his own mind to see things as others do. And even though I don't fully understand the changes of the past several years, I try not to let the children sense my uncertainty.

Our son John tries to be stoic and helpful; that's his nature. He takes on a fatherly role, reading books to Elly at bedtime—something Steve can't always do. Elly, in contrast, is emotional. She cries when upset, and she's especially affected when Steve's paranoia flares and he leaves home unexpectedly. He'll drive the countryside for hundreds of miles, stopping only to buy gas or eat at a fast-food restaurant. He'll park his car facing the road, afraid that someone is following, intent on stopping him from pursuing his cause against SAE. When Steve leaves like this, Elly comes to my bed in tears.

"When is Daddy coming home?" she'll ask. I'll reassure her that it will be soon, and pulling her close, I'll rub her back and stroke her fine blonde hair.

"Take a deep breath and hold it," I'll say, helping her relax. When her breathing evens out and she is asleep again, I'll worry about how Steve's illness will play out in the lives of our children. On many of these nights, I think of Luke, who's had the most trouble accepting Steve's illness. A child with his own challenges—he was diagnosed with ADHD in elementary school and has a learning disability—he did better growing up in an environment with clear-cut rules, where black and white didn't overlap and where sickness and health were separate. Once, when he was in middle school and I was trying to explain his father's behaviors as symptoms of an illness, he shot back: "He could control himself if he wanted to. If you put a gun to his head, he could control himself!"

But I also feel sorry for Steve. The drugs make him lethargic, too uncertain of himself to ask someone for the ketchup. Yet he perseveres in the hope of getting back some of his life. Since Detroit, he regularly visits a psychiatrist and a therapist, and they help him to understand the changes in daily life for people with mental illnesses. Before the appointments, Steve and I prepare a list of questions and concerns about what's happened since his last visit. And because Steve's short-term memory is impaired from both the medications he takes and his altered mental state, we also write down any shifts in moods and thinking the doctor or therapist should know about. He also attends support group meetings, and has participated in vocational retraining through a government program that helps people with disabilities find work. He won't work as an engineer anymore, though; the stress would be too great.

I know that Steve's mind still festers with thoughts about SAE, despite his awareness that he can't act on them. After Detroit, when Steve was discharged from the hospital and came back home to live, we had an unspoken agreement that he would no longer pursue his vendetta against his former employer. "You'll know he's getting better when SAE is no longer important to him," a nurse had told me when he was in the hospital. I often remind him of this.

Yet, in one of the notes he prepared for his therapist, he wrote about his fear of my leaving him if he persisted in his cause: "If I do write the letters [to the board of directors], I think I could work better or look for a job better. Also SAE wouldn't invade my mind when I'm raking leaves, driving the car, or trying to sleep. I went through my SAE box and put my complaints on sheets of paper, [but] I don't think I'll send these because Linda won't put up with it." For years Steve had carefully guarded the information he collected about SAE, which he kept in a cardboard box in his bedroom closet.

Steve watches Elly as she puts ketchup on her burger and fries, placing the bottle back on the table when she's finished.

I soften; he's a good man who's lost so much.

"Pass your dad the ketchup."

Looking up from her plate, Elly grabs the bottle with both hands and hefts it toward her father, who takes it without comment.

Living with a mental illness has changed my life tremendously, but I'm okay, I remind myself, and my family is still intact. "The best-laid plans . . ."

Over the past several years, I've unwittingly crafted my own mantra. I say it often, at times like this, when I feel saddened and overwhelmed: "To get to the end without being bitter." It might not be as poetic as my mother's, but it helps me to persevere.

The Course of the River

Mary Elizabeth Rauktis

O N A WARM AND BRILLIANT OCTOBER AFTERNOON, my mother fell as she crossed the street to the New to You consignment shop, intent on retrieving the cane she'd left behind while browsing. While her body would eventually heal, her mental health would come to resemble that cane: it, too, was a thing she would try to recover but never manage to reclaim. In the months after she tumbled to the cement, her carefully constructed world would shatter like the bones in her hip.

"Who will take care of me?" she asked repeatedly after her surgery. "What will happen to me?" Unable to be reassured or comforted, she wept inconsolably, as if she were suffering from a pain more terrible than the aches brought on by her physical injuries. When this emotional wildfire had finally blazed through her, it was replaced by a depression so profound that there was nothing recognizable of her left. By January the mother I knew—the one who was always looking for a party or to play with Barbies with her granddaughter, the one who could get a complete stranger at a bus stop to tell their life story—

seemed to have already died. In her place sat this elderly stranger, pretending to be my mother. This other-mother didn't smile or laugh; she had no interest in her children or grandchildren; she didn't want to see her friends. Her all-consuming obsession with her physical health convinced her that she was going to die at any moment. I didn't like this other-mother. I wanted my real mother back.

I am a child welfare researcher, and I'm skilled at collecting and analyzing information in order to understand problems. I decided to apply the same method to try to understand what happened to my mother, and what could be done to make her better. My search revealed that about a quarter of geriatric patients die within weeks after a hip fracture, and of those who do survive the surgery and the rehabilitation and physically recover, about a third will become moderately to profoundly depressed. This, in turn, interferes with the person's daily functioning, creating a vicious cycle of depression and physical deterioration that leads, eventually, to death. With a history of depression that began with a hospitalization when she was thirty-five years old, my mother was particularly at risk. This was before I was born, but by talking with my sister, who was about seven at the time, I could piece together some of what had happened to her during that first depression.

My mother had become depressed and delusional, convinced that she was dying, and her functioning deteriorated to the point that she couldn't take care of my sister. There weren't a lot of treatment options available for depression in the 1950s. As was typical treatment for the time, she spent several months in a state hospital and received electroconvulsive therapy (ECT), one of the few available therapies for depression at that time. The ECT worked—she improved and was discharged from the hospital. She would struggle with a chronically low mood throughout her life, but she never had another episode of depression that required hospitalization.

As she aged, however, events she'd previously been able to cope with—a short period of illness, a long and cold winter that kept her confined to her apartment—now seemed to trigger periods of depression and hopelessness. She was on an antidepressant when she broke her hip. It was as if she had been treading water until that day: not reaching the shore, but not drowning, either. She was overwhelmed by the accident, by the tsunami of trauma, surgery, pain, anesthesia, and disrupted routine that followed. She couldn't keep head above the water anymore.

Since I had a medical and research background, my older sister and brother were depending on me to figure out what was going on and what to do. But I could never quite pinpoint whether the depression stemmed from the accident and its subsequent traumas, or whether the event had exacerbated an existing condition. The research did tell us that if we didn't act and get her into the hospital soon, her functioning would continue to deteriorate, and she would probably die. She agreed to go to the hospital, and her doctor admitted her to the psychiatric unit. I hoped that a new medication, perhaps one of the newer classes of anti-depressants, would restore her to a state that resembled the one she was in before she fell.

But not all mental health problems are so easily solved. My brother called me one day to talk about her.

"What do you think? It's been four weeks, and she looks the same—maybe even worse. Why isn't it working?" he asked. I had been wondering the same thing, my concern deepening. And I was feeling guilty. I was the one who had recommended hospitalization.

"I don't know. She's starting to have tics and problems walking. I think it's from the medication—sometimes it has side effects that look like Parkinson's disease."

"What else can they do?" he continued. Underlying the conversation was a shared but unspoken concern: *what if this is what she is going to be like forever?*

"I don't know, but I'll talk to her doctor," I promised. Something had to be done. She had to be fixed.

—

"Your mother isn't responding to the antidepressants," the geriatric psychiatrist said, "and if I increase them any higher, the side effects will get worse. I think a course of bilateral ECT is the next course of action. It can sometimes be effective when medication fails, particularly for the elderly."

"When can you start?" I asked.

The process of ECT involves sedating the patient with general anesthesia and a muscle relaxant, then sending an electrical current through the electrode pads on one or both sides of the head, creating a seizure. Although the causal mechanisms are not fully understood, the procedure is believed to somehow reboot neural functioning in parts of the brain. If changing the chemicals in her brain through medication didn't work, perhaps ECT would restore her nervous system back to something approximating normal. I hoped it would be just a matter of finding the right combination of ECT and medication.

Why did it matter so much? In the past, our relationship had been characterized by my contempt for her helplessness and passivity. I'd wanted her to stand up for herself when my dad bullied her; to have an opinion; to encourage me to leave home, go to medical school, and see the world. She wanted me to be a nurse, have children, and stay in Pittsburgh, preferably within a city block of the family home. She was dismayed by my choice to focus on career rather than family.

Our mutual disappointment in each other was our only common ground for years—until my daughter Olivia was born. My mother loved her extravagantly. She could play with her for hours, helping her to painstakingly dress and accessorize her Barbie dolls; and I know she let Olivia eat cotton candy and Klondike ice cream bars before dinner, because my daughter would confess to me when she later refused to eat. But while I may have complained, I really didn't mind. She was enjoying her granddaughter, and I felt joy in watching this process. I also hoped she might see that I was striving to be a good mother, a better daughter, and a more generous human being. I needed her to get better so we could continue on this path. I wasn't ready to stop, and there was no way I could do it without her.

"We have to fill out these papers; they need them before you have ECT, Mom. They want to know what they're allowed to do if your heart stops." The hospital had asked me to complete her "advance directives," instructions on what they were permitted to do in case she experienced an event, such as a heart attack or stroke, while in the hospital. "Do you want life-sustaining equipment like ventilators and respirators? Do you want them to do CPR on you? What about food and fluids—do you want a feeding tube?"

Even at the time, I recognized the irrationality of asking these questions: her thoughts were so disorganized that she couldn't choose between the cherry Jell-O and the rice pudding on her Presidents Day-themed lunch menu. I watched her gaze out of the window at the snowy park. Her hair, uncombed and flattened in the back from months of lying horizontally, was in desperate need of a trim. She picked at her sweater with her ragged and yellowed nails. I wasn't sure whose sweater she was wearing. I laundered her clothes and returned each item—her initials, "PM," indelibly inked on it—but ownership of clothing appeared to be optional on the psychiatric unit.

"I don't want to be in pain," she said.

"This isn't about pain medication—this is about what you want done if something happens while you're here, if your heart stops and you can't speak for yourself. The hospital wants to know what they are allowed to do," I repeated.

Impatient, I looked down and scanned the ranked options for keeping someone alive, checking "no" for feeding tubes and respirators, "yes" for minimal actions like IVs and blood, wishing all the while that one of my siblings was having this conversation instead of me. I am the youngest. Why wasn't birth order working in my favor? I resented the hours I'd spent watching her sit and stare sightlessly out of the window overlooking the emergency helicopter pad, time taken away from my students and work, hours stolen from my husband and daughter. I wondered if she even wanted to be alive, and the thought filled me with equal parts of rage and resentment. She has a good life, one worth fighting for, I thought, and she doesn't care. How could she give up so easily? She just wasn't trying hard enough.

"I don't want to be in pain . . . I don't care what you let them do to me, but promise me that you won't let me suffer," she said.

It was the most coherent sentence she had spoken in months, and she looked at me—really looked at me—for the first time since she'd broken her hip. I wondered if the frustration, resentment, and anger that had been building up in me over the past four months were now so evident that she feared I would let her suffer as punishment.

"I won't let you suffer," I said, giving the assurance as casually as if I had promised to bring her favorite slippers from home. I had no idea how difficult this promise would be to keep.

The ECT did give her a period of remission from the depression, but the window of time was short. We watched a lot of TV together during that brief period, especially the game show Jeopardy. Ken Jennings, who would ultimately go undefeated for seventy-four consecutive games, was the reigning champion, and she enthusiastically rooted against him, loudly urging the other contestants, particularly the women, to "kick his butt." I enjoyed watching her cheer for the underdogs—my mother, the late-blooming feminist. It was something new, and fun to see.

Nothing specific happened to cause her depression to reoccur, but within ten months she was back on the psychiatric unit. Each time I saw her she was less engaged, more internally focused on her anxiety, sadness, pain, and fear for what would happen to her. More disturbing, she was becoming increasingly confused. She realized this, and it increased her anxiety exponentially.

I could hear her sobbing when I was buzzed through the locked doors that led to the psychiatric unit. She was always sitting next to the nurses station, where the nurses parked all the "problem" geriatric patients in their wheelchairs in order to keep an eye on them. In my mother's case, it was her confusion and anxiety that made her a problem and a falling risk. My petite mother could slip, Houdini-like, out of the more comfortable vest restraints, so they had to use wrist restraints instead. Her wrists were bruised from her pulling at them, as were her heels, which she would bang against the wheelchair's metal footrests. The nurses regularly apologized for the restraints, explaining, "We have to do that or she will get up and fall. She's so agitated, so confused. Nothing is helping to calm her down." Medication did not help, and her ECT was discontinued because it only increased her confusion and agitation. There was nothing to be done but send her to a long-term dementia unit in a nursing home. She couldn't be fixed.

I was losing my mother and failing to keep my promise. And my belief in the empirical process of medicine, its ability to diagnose and cure, was deeply shaken. I wasn't letting her suffer due to my anger, but because of my incompetence. I couldn't figure out what was wrong. No matter how much I pored over the research, looking for descriptions of this blend of agitation, confusion and depression, I couldn't solve the problem. I could no longer concentrate at work, either, my sole refuge, and I began to think that maybe I, too, was losing my mind. I needed some help.

"So you made a promise that she wouldn't suffer. What makes you believe that you have the power to prevent suffering, pain? Are you God?" The therapist to whom I'd been assigned had quickly become directive during our second session. "You no more have the power to change this situation than you have to alter the course of the Ohio River. We all want an easy death, but no human has the power to grant that wish. Get over that delusion, grieve, and find a way to make your peace with this situation."

This was tough. It would not be so easy to give up the delusion that I could control the circumstances of her death. Yet it also relieved me of some of the guilt that had made it difficult to be with her—and equally difficult to be away from her.

I still hadn't accepted the situation when, one November evening, I was sitting next to her bed in the nursing home, looking out the window at the abrupt fall of darkness that happens after turning back the clocks. She awoke, looked at me, and said, "Mary, you need to go home; you have a long way to drive and it's dark and Olivia will be wondering where you are." I realize now that she was giving me permission to get on with my life. I didn't know that it would be the last time my mother would speak directly to me, using my name.

My mother died on a brilliant and cold January afternoon while in hospice. I received the call at work, and after calling my brother and sister, I made a quick stop at home before walking to the corner where the school bus would drop off Olivia. We walked home together.

Choke

Zoë Hooley

"**I**'LL BE LOCKING UP YOUR POSSESSIONS. In a few days we'll see about putting you back in your own clothes. Cell phones are not permitted on the unit; get out any numbers you may need. There are payphones in the common area that you can use after breakfast and before dinner. There are walk-throughs every fifteen minutes—for your safety." The monotony of the nurse's voice showed that she had given this speech countless times. "Do you have any questions?"

I mutely shook my head. I did have a question: Could I get out of here? But I already knew the answer. We sat in a tiny room, just big enough for two chairs and an old metal desk that looked as worn as I felt.

"Before I take you to your room, I need to do a skin check."

"A what?"

"I need to check for any existing marks or wounds. If you can stand up?" she coaxed, clicking her pen.

I rose and reluctantly lifted my hospital gown as she dutifully noted my scars on the genderless diagram on her clipboard, a personal paint-by-number. She scribbled a mark for the bird tattoo on my ribs, the scar from the mole I'd had removed from my arm when I was fifteen, the birthmark on my left calf.

"Turn around."

I complied, feeling a twinge of shame as she marked down the phoenix tattoo I'd gotten three years earlier, after I'd almost killed myself. (The first time, my planned defenestration. Not to be confused with when I almost killed myself this time.) Wings spread wide in flight, as if about to soar off my shoulder, it symbolized how suffering begets rebirth. Where was resurrection now? I felt nothing but the flat pile of ashes, smelled nothing but smolder.

"All done," she said with a reassuring smile.

The nurse took me down the hall, past the many whiteboards affixed to doorways like placards. She paused at one with a vacancy and wrote in my name—my first name, the one only my grandma calls me—along with the names of my assigned nurse and social worker.

"I'll give you a few minutes to get settled," she said, gesturing toward the bed and nightstand that together occupied half of the room; a curtain separated them from an identical arrangement on the other side. The built-in furniture reminded me of the dorms in college, the ones in the old residence hall. "I'll check on when the doctor will see you."

I sat tentatively on the bed, numbness and emotion vying for dominance. They'd been playing tug-of-war for the last several days, but I could *feel* that emotion was going to win this one. Which is to say, I could feel. Anxiety and fear and frustration bumped into each other in my stomach, looking for a way out. I searched in the paper grocery-turned-duffel bag I'd used to carry my things from the downstairs crisis unit, rummaging for my journal and a pencil. Pens, for reasons as inscrutable as my breakdown, were considered potential weapons and weren't allowed.

I was interrupted as a short, middle-aged woman with a wide face and wider smile shuffled into the room on the blue socks that everyone wore in the unit. I was sniffing back my tears as she noticed me sitting on the bed.

"Are you in my room?"

I nodded shyly, not trusting that my voice would be clear of tears.

"I'm Cynthia." Her guilelessness and my self-doubt did a tango around the room.

"Hi, Cynthia."

"We're watching TV." It was an assumption more than an invitation. Of course everyone wants to watch TV.

"I think I have to wait for the nurse."

"Oh, okay." She started to leave the room, then turned back. "I've got grapes."

A grin punctured my numbness. "I'm okay."

Five days ago, I'd been rushed to the ER with a dangerously high blood alcohol level.

A break up on the heels of a move on the heels of a job-change—to think about it made my head spin and my stomach ache. So I tried not to.

I came home from work to my Chicago apartment, empty except for Raymond, the beta fish, who wasn't much of a conversationalist. I started drinking—just to take the edge off. But the edge was deep and jagged and I slipped into it. Alcohol was a recent addition to my strategies for quelling my chronic, throbbing anxiety. Running too much, cleaning too long (and then cleaning again), eating too little: I'd tried my hand at them all. But none had been able to stop the pulsing dread more than whiskey. A lightweight, I quickly outpaced myself, and by the time my roommate got home, I was breathing threats—wishes, perhaps—of suicide.

"I slapped you. I'm sorry," she told me later. "I wanted you to snap out of it." But I'd already snapped.

—

The ambulance clattered and howled through the streets of Chicago, me in its belly. They wouldn't let my roommate ride in the ambulance; they wouldn't let me leave the hospital. Involuntary commitment is called "C&P" in Illinois: Certificate and Petition. As much as I petitioned, they wouldn't let me leave.

I spent the next several days in the crisis unit, waiting for an open bed in the psychiatric ward six floors above. They answered the phone by saying, "Crisis." It was the ward's official greeting. Emergencies were standard.

My first morning upstairs in the psych unit, they woke me at 6:10 a.m. to take blood. I rubbed the sleep out of my eyes as the nurse rubbed an alcohol swab on my forearm.

"There will be a little poke," she narrated as she lifted the needle. I barely noticed, my drowsiness serving as an anesthetic.

"That wasn't so bad, huh?" she said cheerily, removing the tourniquet. I smiled absently as she gathered her supplies and left the room, calling, "Breakfast will be up soon!" as she departed.

I caught sight of myself in the mirror as I made my way to the bathroom. My curly hair looked as if it had been practicing gymnastics all night, and my eyes had a glassy pre-coffee blankness. The baggy blue hospital gown drifted around me as if it wasn't sure what to do, either. I hesitated for a moment, listless, before impulsively burrowing in my bag for my lipstick, dabbing on the color quickly and decisively. I nodded at my reflection before heading down the hallway to the dining room.

My eyes scanned the three rows of tables with all the certainty of a new kid who'd just walked into an unfamiliar cafeteria. On the far side of the room, Cynthia was motioning to me. When she caught my eye, she patted a spot beside her at the table. I angled my way there. When I sat down, she introduced me to her neighbor.

"This is Zoë. She's my new roommate." I tried to focus, to absorb their names, but my brain was such a tangle, and nothing sunk in.

Bill? Marsha? Or was it Martha?

We groggily waited in silence for the staff to distribute the food. Our meals came up to the unit in a big capsule of molded plastic, which made a sound like the opening bay doors of a spaceship when they unlatched it. The trays were covered with plastic domes resembling flying saucers, orbited by tiny satellites of orange juice and reduced-sodium margarine.

I scooted the breakfast sausage to the outskirts of my plate. They remembered I was a vegetarian about 45 percent of the time. No matter: they had sent coffee. I slurped it as eagerly and gingerly as if it were real coffee—from one of the upscale boutiques in the Gold Coast that I passed every day on my way to work—and not bland, burnt Folgers.

As I sipped, my gaze roamed around the room. The other patients were trading items from their trays like baseball cards.

"Ronald, you can have my juice."

"Anyone want my biscuit?"

"Give your jam to Gina, she always likes it."

The patients whose medication made them prone to dizziness wore yellow socks—bright yellow—cluing in the staff to the fact that they were unstable. But weren't we all? Wasn't that why we were in the psych ward?

Later, I lay in my bed, trying to clear space in my head for sleep. I wondered if my brother was trying to get ahold of me. I wondered how I would explain my absence to my boss. I had called into work, earlier that day, and made as vague an excuse for my hospitalization as I could muster. Brian answered the phone. We call him The Beast. After I'd broken up with my boyfriend, Brian offered to beat him up. (He then went on to relate tales of all the people he'd beaten up already—there were many.) Brian sounded so scared, saying he was worried sick about me. Why hadn't I called? He spoke quickly and nervously, like a child. I was one of Brian's favorites, the only girl in the back stock crew. He'd chosen me because he thought me capable and strong. But here I was in the psych ward. Regret and shame frayed the edges of my thoughts.

Feet could be heard making their way down the tiled hallway.

"Just a safety check." Came a cheerful voice from the doorway. "Everything okay?"

"Yeah," Cynthia piped up from the far side of the room. "I'm gonna choke her when you leave though," she said around giggles.

Stillness returned to the room after the nurse left.

"I wasn't really going to choke you, you know," Cynthia said from the darkness on the other side of the curtain.

Three days later, my gathered things—a drawing by my friend's three-year-old, sent to cheer me; the wilting flowers my friend Joseph had brought; the social worker's card—jutted out of the grocery bag, now torn at one corner from use.

Cynthia had left the day before. I had suggested that maybe we could swap addresses and write. It's what I'd learned to say to departing cabinmates at summer camp.

"I'm not too good with words," she hedged, taking the pencil. Her face wrinkled with concentration, the paper wrinkling under her measured hand, she made up with force what she lacked in finesse. I slipped the address into my journal alongside other valuables: a pressed flower, my prescription for antidepressants.

"Would you help me fill this out?" Cynthia asked, holding out a form. I nodded quickly—too quickly—eager to jump over any gap where embarrassment might insert itself. I read the questions to her slowly, slipping into the voice my mother used for story time.

The next day, I answered the questions for myself:

During this hospital stay, how often were your room and bathroom kept clean?
D. Always
During this hospital stay, how often did nurses treat you with courtesy and respect?

C. Usually
During this hospital stay, how often did doctors listen carefully to you?
B. Sometimes
Would you recommend this hospital to your friends and family?
B. Probably no. (It depends on their roommate.)
In general, how would you rate your overall mental or emotional health?
Fair, gathering wind.

It would take days and weeks and years before I could use "health" to classify my emotional state, but I could hear in the distance the rustle of wings. A plume from the pyre, the phoenix flies.

Blood Work

Yona Harvey

I LOCK MY OFFICE DOOR, TAKE A FEW DEEP BREATHS, and turn the pages of Brandi's journal. It's the fullest personal record of my sister's life, the only one I found while cleaning and packing her Chicago condominium. I'd recognized it immediately by the Jacob Lawrence painting, *The Library*, reproduced on the front and back covers. I'd given Brandi the journal to celebrate her first birthday away at college. When I found it, our parents were packing up in other rooms, and I quickly shoved it into my purse. Brandi would not, I convinced myself, have wanted our parents reading her journal. Besides, what if she'd written something critical of them? They wouldn't be able to handle it.

Mostly the journal is an account of Brandi's first year on campus at The Ohio State University, filled with predictable gripes about classes, dorm mates, and new love interests. Her journal also reveals, though, bouts of depression, stress, insecurity, and suicidal thoughts, as well as her visits to a campus therapist. The 1994–1995 academic year was a challenging period for my sister. It was her first

time away from home, and she was baffled by the social life, contra-
dictions, and new ideas that many college students face. Not long
after Thanksgiving 1995, she writes:

GOOD THINGS
M. looks up to me—school—change[d] her major to business (accounting)
R. looks up to me—I encouraged her to stay in college
Yona looks up to me—personality
My family looks up to me
i.e. college
M. loves me
His family loves me
L. loves me
His family loves me
Granny loves me
Think about D.J.
L.E.

I believe Langston Hughes when he writes that "poems, like prayers,
possess power," and I read what Brandi writes as a poem. Brandi's
poem has a title, line breaks, and an affirming catalog of "good
things" that ends with the name of a teenaged boy, L.E., who once
captured Brandi's imagination. Maybe because I'm a poet and an
older sister wanting peace of mind, I can't help but read Brandi's
work this way. I want to believe that Brandi's catalog of good things
pulled her back from isolation. And I'm relieved to know that, for
one year at least, Brandi found some comfort in writing and record-
ing her thoughts, and that she sought help for her depression and
difficulties. What she writes is part poem, part affirmation, part girl
talk, and part secret. And, like Brandi, the poem keeps certain information to itself. Who, for instance, was D.J.? The name doesn't ring
the slightest bell.

Her sloppy handwriting and cryptic, graffiti-like tags—"college
life," "snap," "fuck da bullshit"—make me feel connected to Brandi

once more, binding us together again as two sisters who gossiped and vented in my high school bedroom with the door shut. But the journal also makes me wonder why Brandi never told me about feeling depressed. She was my most trusted friend, the maid of honor at my wedding, my closest living ancestor. Did she feel ashamed of her depression or the inner workings of her brain? Did my parents and I pressure Brandi with too many expectations? If I hadn't become distracted by the demands of marriage and mothering, would Brandi have called me for help sooner—long before she found herself running from an ER examination room to peer over the ledge of a hospital garage roof?

"Sometimes I think I'm slow," she writes on one page of her journal, as if people were born hip and charming, as if the young women and men around her were pulling things off better. She didn't hide what she didn't know; she was incapable of such posturing. What she didn't know, though, sometimes embarrassed her.

Reading the journal, I search for the one clue that will erase all mystery, the sentence that says, "On this day, at this time, such and such happened and put me over the edge." I look for any hint that predicts how Brandi might have felt during the last week of her life. And when I can't find helpful clues from that period, I hunt further back, trying to locate some revealing thing about the way my sister and I grew up, how we lived, who we befriended, what we ate—anything that might help me to understand Brandi's anguish. I can never dissect Brandi's brain, examine her body, or take blood samples. And Brandi's journal is a fragmented record, with time gaps. Her entire adulthood is missing. Brandi was thirty years old when she died—far from the freshman college student who wrote these pages. Perhaps my clinging to these pages makes no sense. But as the sound of Brandi's voice, her scent, and the tightness of her hugs fade, these tactile pages remain. Years past Brandi's death, I'm relying primarily on memory; but turning the pages, I commit to the difficult work of unearthing the mysteries of my sister, my kin, my blood.

—

It's early April 2007 in Cincinnati, Ohio, a few days after Easter. It's the season of children's recitations of Bible verses, family dinners with glazed hams and green beans with potatoes, ritual prayers by the faithful for the sick and shut-in. Sinners who've drifted return home to Zion for the pastor's retelling of Christ's resurrection, that quintessential Christian sermon. My mother, recently retired as a secretary from Proctor & Gamble, has become an ordained Pentecostal minister. And though she doesn't yet know it, this week will mark the beginning of the insomnia that will plague her for the next several years.

"I'm stressed out," Brandi will often say before growing silent, starting to weep, or falling to the living room floor of our parents' condominium to pound the carpet with her fists. When my parents and I ask, "What's wrong?" this is always her sole explanation. When she isn't crying or curled in a heap, she wanders from room to room with a distant look on her face. She breaks her silences with what appear to be newly surfaced memories, rattling off time-warped sentences like a broken doll with a worn and tangled string on her back. "You need to learn to love yourself," she says, grabbing and shaking the bedpost in our parents' room. "You need to learn to love yourself," she repeats, mimicking, it seems, someone else's harsh criticism. Or, perhaps, her own?

Her shiny black hair is wound in two-strand twists, slightly frayed at the ends. She's dressed in a T-shirt and sweatpants; anyone might mistake her for a college undergraduate. With the exception of her hair, which she changes frequently, Brandi looks the same as when our mother saw her last: she has the clear, amber skin of a person who doesn't drink, smoke, or eat much junk food. Before walking away, she stops, turns, and faces our mother.

"Did he put his hands on you?"

Her question bears a startling mystery and soundness. Did who put his hands on her? Brandi resumes her meandering without waiting for an answer.

Our mother follows Brandi from room to room; and after several hours, she calls me. "She won't calm down," she says, shortly after midnight, whispering into the phone so Brandi won't overhear. "She doesn't want to be alone, and she doesn't want me to run any water."

"Chicago is not my home," Brandi says, correcting the ER nurse who reviews her insurance and contact information. This morning, our mother gave Brandi a bath and brushed her hair, just as she'd done when Brandi was little. Brandi hasn't slept much, but she is calm and waits quietly for her assigned doctor. In her medical records, we will later see, the nurse describes Brandi's voice as despondent and "flat," noting that the patient says she is "stressed." He directs Brandi and our parents to the seating area.

The Christ Hospital is where our parents met as teenagers, earning their first real-world paychecks by delivering food trays to patients. Granny, my father's mother, retired from food service here and lives a few blocks away. The hospital rests in the heart of Mount Auburn, a neglected, predominantly black neighborhood that was once the home of William Howard Taft. In recent years, white city residents searching for cheap property near the University of Cincinnati have ventured as far as Granny's street, the first signs of inevitable gentrification.

After a few hours, the nurse calls Brandi's name and takes her to the examination room, our parents following softly behind.

"If you don't want to be here," the nurse says, handing Brandi a paper, "you can complete this form and be released." Brandi writes her name, then hesitates. She crumples the paper.

The doctor will introduce himself and seem, my parents will say, slightly bothered by what he assesses as Brandi's lack of cooperation. Does the doctor have any experience with mentally ill patients? Do the doctor's questions about physical ailments reflect his inattention to Brandi's mental health? Does the doctor find it strange that my parents have accompanied their thirty-year-old daughter to the ER? Does the white doctor have prejudices about the black population of Mount Auburn? If so, to what degree are these prejudices at work? Does the doctor believe mentally ill patients have a certain physical appearance? That they speak a certain way? Behave a certain way? Should attending ER physicians have a list of questions that address mental health care? These are some of the questions I'll formulate during the next several months. These are the questions I've asked again and again and again. And each day without Brandi I answer: yes, yes, yes.

Here's what will be undisputed: The doctor's phone will ring. He'll take the call and leave the room.

After a while, Brandi will fidget; she'll ask if the doctor will be back soon.

And then, the action that will puzzle and haunt everyone forever: Brandi will run. She will run like an Olympic medal is within her grasp, like her legs are made of bionic parts, like the Hellhounds are on her trail. A knees-up, pumped-up bolt.

The thirty-something doctor with wire-rimmed glasses and thinning blonde hair will return to my mother to ask if our family has any history of mental health issues. His question will be too late.

Brandi is throwing a housewarming party at her condo on Chicago's South Side; my mother, father, grandmother, and I arrive a day early to spend more time with her. Though my sister bought her condo over a year ago, her rooms have few accessories and no paintings or pictures on the still-white walls. Her furniture consists of a small kitchen table, a modest sofa, a few chairs. Our footsteps echo as we walk along the hardwood floors.

Brandi's condo is the exact opposite of my home in Pittsburgh, where I trip over toys, cram books and magazines into corners, and greet another person in every room. My attention bounces precipitously among my husband, Terrance; my three-year-old son; my seven-year-old daughter; an unfinished poetry manuscript; and an intense graduate program in library and information science. Brandi and I share the nasty habit of doing too much at once. So I feel relieved to be simply a sister and daughter again, however briefly. I suspect Brandi feels this relief, too. Her friend who was supposed to help with party planning cancels at the last minute, and Brandi instantly puts my mother and me to work. We land at Target, searching for napkins, paper plates, and air mattresses, and despite the upcoming party tomorrow, we easily fall back into our familiar, carefree disregard for time.

"What do you think about these pants?" I ask Brandi.

She turns up her nose. "I don't buy clothes at Target."

"Forget you," I say, fake-elbowing her. "Married mothers of two on a budget shop at Target." I can hardly stop smiling. I'm proud of Brandi, all grown up and living what I perceive to be a "cool, single life" in the big city, a funds manager at Northern Trust Bank who has modeled in hair shows for neighborhood salons. She has new friends from her church and job, some of whom will attend the party. A few co-workers have been trying to fix Brandi up with "the new guy" from the UK, but she's not interested. He, too, will be at the party, and I'm eager to size him up.

Back home, I'm swimming to stay afloat and maintain an independent identity, which seems to multiply with each commitment, childbirth, and family move. Maybe this is why I can't see Brandi's loneliness. I often long to be alone, taking for granted the built-in support around me—my son's fingers curled around my hair, my daughter's framed artwork, Terrance's affections—human touches. I do not imagine how strange it might be for Brandi to hear only the echo of her own footsteps and, perhaps, the murmur of television voices at the end of the day.

I'm speeding south on Interstate 71, passing the city limits of Columbus, Ohio, the last segment of the drive to Cincinnati from my house in Pittsburgh. I feel the air leave the car, the swift pressure of a tight squeeze around my arms and chest, and then the ghost thump of drums. Why can't I breathe? Joan Osborne slips through the stereo speakers with her blues brand of Bob Dylan's "Man in the Long Black Coat": "she's gone, she's gone." Only a moment ago, at the side of the road, I played a voicemail message from Aunt Nellie, my mother's sister.

"Come to Christ Hospital," she said. "Get here as soon as you can."

She didn't answer when I called back. Why was she calling me when she knew I was already on my way to meet Brandi and my parents? And why am I even listening to this music? At the last minute, I grabbed the CD from an old box of forgotten discs, not wanting to waste time, having no memory of this song or its lyrics. Did I tune out Brandi in a similar way? Hearing only what I wanted? Hearing only what felt neat and good?

I was up most of the night, the result of my mother calling every two hours or so in a panic about Brandi, whose behavior has become increasingly erratic this past week.

"I'm afraid of who's waiting there," I told Terrance a few hours ago, placing my toothbrush on the bathroom counter. He stood behind me, wearing his glasses, his six-foot-six, former-college-basketball-player body barely fitting the mirror's frame.

"It's gonna be fine," he said, rubbing my shoulders. "And it's not about you; it's about your family. They need you." But he wasn't familiar with the Brandi of late, the inconsolable one. He hadn't heard Brandi's voice, high-pitched and euphoric one minute, flat and emotionless the next. He knew Brandi as he last saw her: five foot eight and bubbly, Halle Berry haircut, blasting Fantasia songs on her laptop, modeling the winter coat our parents gave her for Christmas, a complete ham sandwich as she mocked the catwalk swag of a high-profile, high-fashion diva.

"OK, love you, bye," she'd said on the phone, yesterday afternoon, like an automaton asking a customer to hold for the next available agent. It would be the last time I'd hear her speak.

No one will catch Brandi. Not the medical staff, not the baffled onlookers, not the team of security personnel, and not my father, for whom Brandi breaks stride for just a second, near an exit that leads to the parking garage roof. "You said they would help me," she shouts, before turning and running away.

What is the language of anguish? What did Brandi mean when she confessed she felt "slow"? What happened to Brandi during the time when she wasn't writing, in the years between college graduation and her work for a major banking company? What happens when a woman struggles to find words for the strangeness of her mind? When Brandi told our parents, her co-workers, the emergency room personnel, and me that she was "stressed," so much depended upon what each of us could hear.

"She jumped on that ledge so fast," my father will tell me days before the funeral, "like Superwoman. Before she went over, her coat brushed my hand."

Winter Break

Lauren Shapiro

IT WAS NINE O'CLOCK ON CHRISTMAS MORNING, and I was putting on my bathing suit at the Rincón Beach Resort in Puerto Rico when my phone rang.

"Dad's gone again," my sister said. "He left another note."

A tunnel opened up inside my head and began sucking up everything in the room: the torn gift wrap on the floor, the scattered toys, my husband, Kevin, who was struggling to get our one-year-old son into swim trunks.

"What did it say?" I managed.

"That it was no one's fault." I hung up and collapsed onto the bed.

"He's going to do it this time," I said, the tears coming on now.

Kevin paced the room. "The fuck were they thinking, calling you?" he yelled. He picked up his phone and began to text my sister.

"Stop, stop, stop," I said, burrowing in deeper. The room was the tunnel, and I was part of it. The boundaries of objects evaporated.

"We're two thousand miles away! It's Christmas!" he said. "What the fuck do they want you to do? Sit and cry in a hotel room?"

"He's doing it," I said. "I know!"

"No, he's not. He doesn't have the balls."

I was suddenly aware of our son, Javi, half dressed and clutching a pacifier in each hand, staring at us. Had I ever cried in front of him? I wiped my face.

Because there was nothing else to do, we went down to the pool.

Our friends Dan and Becca, just married, had joined us for Christmas, along with my in-laws, who live in Puerto Rico. Kevin's parents had divorced, but the birth of Javi, their only child's son, seemed to have brought them closer together. The resort was small, a hotel really, but the pool sat right next to the beach and featured a small and very infrequently staffed bar. There was a kiddy pool, a hot tub, a giant chess board, a ping-pong table without paddles.

The place was almost empty, save for another family that I recognized from yesterday. Kevin had pointed out their little girl, roughly four years old, who'd refused to let Javi play with her toys. "That girl will grow up to be what we call a *comemierda*," he'd said, "a spoiled brat. Just look at her." She was dressed similarly today: a sparkly pink bathing suit, matching water shoes, elaborate hair bows, a glittery star sticker stuck to her cheek. And she was surrounded by intricate water toys: boats with removable plastic people and doors that opened and shut, large dolphins and whales that squeaked and spouted water, a floating island with palm trees and a treasure chest. I set Javi down next to his own paltry selection: a cheap plastic boat, a few squirt toys. He immediately went for the girl's dolphin.

"Mami, no! It's mine! He can't play with it!" the girl whined in Spanish, looking at her mother and pointing at my son. My phone rang. I let Kevin deal with Javi.

"He's alive," my sister said matter-of-factly. "Dan found him on a ledge at the top of the Air Rights Garage. He pulled him in and held him until the police arrived."

I pictured my slender twenty-six-year-old brother dragging our father over the concrete divide of the garage and pinning him to the asphalt. Less than a month before, on his previous attempt, my father had gone to that very same spot. He'd left a note at home then, too, and while Kevin and I and the police raced around New Haven—looking for his car, trying to track his phone, texting and calling him endlessly—he was trying to find places from which to jump: the bridge (under construction), an icy lake, and finally the ten-flight Air Rights Garage. After nearly six hours, something—I can't imagine what—must have clicked off in his mind, and he turned the key in his car's ignition and descended the ramps out of the garage. When he got home, he stumbled out of the car with a Ziploc bag in his right hand, his wallet sealed inside it. He'd be committed to the very hospital where he worked as a pediatrician. They'd only keep him for three nights.

Kevin and I had just moved from Madison, Wisconsin, to Hartford, Connecticut, and it was a move I was beginning to regret. After a few difficult months of living with my parents, we'd rushed into buying a house we couldn't afford; Javi was not taking well to daycare; and I was busy teaching at a local college and working through the final edits on my first book. Our move to Hartford had been influenced, in part, by the idea of being closer to my parents after Javi's birth. But distance had perhaps led me to minimize the depths of their issues with mental illness, and I soon found myself thrust suddenly into this caretaker role, striving as best I could to bring an elusive happiness and order to their complicated psyches. My siblings, both of whom live in California ("I wonder why!" Kevin would joke), had come to Connecticut for the holidays so we could take a break. For the past five months, I'd been looking forward to nothing more than sitting on the beach and reading gossip magazines, of playing with Javi in the sand, of sipping piña coladas with our friends.

Dan came on the phone and related today's scene: "I snuck up behind him and just bear-hugged him, started yelling, 'Dad, it's me, Dan!' He tried to unzip his jacket. He told me to let go, that he'd come back in. I was like, 'Are you fucking kidding me?' I don't know how, but I just pulled him over and started yelling for the police, who were on the ground. I just held him until they came up." He was breathless, pumped.

"Are *you* all right?" I asked.

"*Me?*" he said. "Are you kidding? I'm a fucking rock. I'm fine."

By the time I got back to the pool, the little girl had moved all of her toys back up to her lounge chair, and Javi was paddling around with Kevin. Our friends were in the pool as well, along with Kevin's mother. His father had come down from his room and was parked at the bar, smoking a cigarette. The bartender, as usual, was nowhere to be found.

"Hello?" Kevin's father yelled. "Anybody? Should I just get behind there and make myself a drink?"

Eventually a young man sidled in behind the bar and nodded.

"Cuba libre," Kevin's father said.

It started to rain. I sat beside him at the bar and ordered a scotch on the rocks.

The mother of a close friend of mine had been diagnosed the previous week with Parkinson's disease, and another friend's father had recently entered hospice with a terminal case of colon cancer. These were terrible illnesses, the parent wasting away, not wanting to go. Despite the emotional toll this must take, it seemed to me an uncomplicated kind of mourning—two people wrested away by a body's breakdown. People offered public condolences, posted on Facebook. I had told next to no one about what was happening to my family, what had been slowly and painfully happening for months and months, during which I had been desperate to fix things. I brought my son to see my father at every opportunity, called my father's psychologists and psychiatrists with worried anecdotes, confronted my mother about her needy behavior, scanned lengthy articles on the Internet, planned elaborate family trips we all knew would never happen. If my father had been diagnosed with a physical illness, even a terminal one, I could have accepted it, been open with people about it.

Instead, I took his recovery onto myself, feeling acutely and privately responsible. If only I did this, if only I did that. Was he in a slightly better mood today? Could I somehow get my infant son to lift his spirits? It was a never-ending dance, an impossible choreography, and he wasn't even looking. Month after month, my father had wanted to die, had been obsessed with it, but he was still here—wasn't he? "You kids kept him alive," my mother had said. "You're the reason he couldn't bring himself to do it." But was this a blessing or a curse? Had we been his saviors, or had we been some kind of tragic impediment, willing him to remain alive in endless, guilty misery?

My father had been the oldest of five, but only three were left. One of my uncles had been schizophrenic and off his medication, and had asphyxiated himself with a plastic bag in his early twenties. Terrible as this was, there was a medical explanation, a diagnosed illness with a name and an appropriate course of action that had not, tragically, been followed. Another uncle, Danny, had fallen prey to a more complicated depressive illness. Afterward, they'd found lists—pages and pages long—of everything he'd felt he needed to accomplish in a given day. Clearly, there was a deep obsessive streak, perhaps OCD, like my father suffered from. Danny had apparently paced back and forth on a bridge in San Francisco for hours before throwing himself off, landing on a red playground slide below.

In both cases my grandfather had visited his sons several days before their deaths, assuring everyone when he left that they were fine. How is this lack of awareness possible? Had my grandfather done all he could? Had he unknowingly pressured his sons into feigning health? There is something mystical about the force of positive thinking, that dull beacon of hope that gets people through difficult times. On the flip side is the blade, the willful ignorance that keeps someone from seeing the terrible reality in front of them.

After his second suicide attempt, my father was diagnosed with a severe form of agitated depression that had been worsened by the high dosage of Prozac he was taking. He'd padlocked his computer in an attempt to keep the CIA away from his investment information, and he was convinced that the American Medical Association was on the brink of revoking his medical license because he'd written himself a prescription, left unfilled, for tranquilizers. My mother caught him looking at website articles with names like "How many Tylenol does it take to kill yourself?" and "How to commit suicide but make it look like an accident," which prompted one of many phone calls to his doctors. My parents had been having serious relationship issues after my mother's own semi-breakdown seven months earlier. On Father's Day, two weeks before Kevin, Javi, and I were supposed to move in with them (and as we searched for more permanent lodging), she'd sent a rambling, incoherent email to us, her children, explaining that her marriage was a sham and that she had taken enough pills to kill herself. When I couldn't reach her, I called 911; the police found her hiding in my father's room. My father was on vacation in Turkey with my brother, and when I Skyped with them to tell them that Mom had been taken to the ER, they appeared onscreen in a cave à la Osama bin Laden hideout. Stalactites dripped in the dim background of the screen, and my father's bearded face hovered in the abyss.

"Jesus, where are you?" I asked.

"In a cave hotel in Cappadocia—asleep," he said.

"Did you get my email?" I said quickly. "Mom's on her way to the ER."

There was a pause. "What do you want me to do about it?" he said flatly. "You know she's always creating drama."

I was stunned. What did I want him to do about it? I guessed I wanted him to come home immediately, as I was living halfway across the country with a six-month-old, a job, a house to sell, and a move to prepare for. They did come home, of course, and indeed it all turned out to be a hysterical, desperate plea for attention on my mother's part. The damage had been done, though—my father slipped into a deep depression as he sifted through the wreckage of his perennially unhealthy marriage, the loss of his brothers, his dwindling place at work, his lack of future prospects.

What was going through my father's head in the months of deep depression and despair before his suicide attempts? What had led him to leave the hospital the first time, assuring everyone he was fine, all the while planning a second attempt? He had emailed my mother, the first time, a one-liner that said, simply, "Look in the bag behind the computer." There my mother found a brief suicide note that my father later admitted to having put there months before. How had he gone about his days, seeing patients, getting dinner with us, playing hollowly with my son, all the while desperately hatching these plans? I can't know what my father was feeling, but it must have been comprised of blinding terror, guilt, self-hatred and wells of despair I can't begin to fathom. Whatever it was had taken him not only from us, his family, but also from himself.

My father has never been one to discuss more than pleasantries and mundane daily details, even with his children. He will chide me for not maintaining adequate records for tax write-offs or ask what my son has done that day. If you try to ask him a question—about work, about how he's feeling—the answer is always "fine." Once, though, a few years ago, he was driving me back to the airport at the end of a visit so I could fly back to graduate school. The air had been mostly dead, the car silent for much of the drive, neither of us offering much, as was our way.

Suddenly he said, "You know, I've carried a lot of guilt since my brothers' deaths."

We were two minutes from the airport, and in the shock of the moment, all I could do was offer a generic remark.

"Even though it's not your fault, it must be really hard to live with that."

We pulled up to the terminal, and I got out of the car. I was shocked by my father's sudden admission, so unlike him. He'd recently started therapy, so I guessed that this must have been one of the first things they'd talked about. But as I sat at the gate, rethinking everything I could have said, I became irritated. Why had he chosen *that* moment to delve into such deep psychological terrain when I'd been visiting for two weeks? In retrospect, could I have done something then to steer him on a different path? Maybe this had been his way of beginning to crack through his wall of pleasantries, the artificial bubble that seemed to envelop him wherever he went: *I'm fine*, that almost religious family refrain.

I spent Christmas afternoon getting drunk on the beach in the rain as my husband and our friends gingerly followed suit. My mother-in-law had taken our son in for his nap, and Kevin's father had gone to his room. After my fifth scotch, things didn't seem less dreary or strange, but I was laughing a little wildly now.

"Hey guys, look at that couple—they must be on their honeymoon—how cliché!" I said loudly, pointing to a guy and girl in their twenties who had buried each other in the sand. "There goes the *comemierda*!" I said, as the family with the little girl packed up their things, looking at us strangely.

"Shhh," Kevin said. "Hey, maybe you should slow down a little?"

"Why? It's fucking Christmas. We're on a tropical island. Didn't we come here to have fun? What's wrong with you guys?" I said. "Another round?" Our friends were smiling a bit nervously, clearly caught in something they hadn't bargained for.

"I might just have a water," Becca said. "Can I get you one, Lauren?"

"Oh God," I said. It was all hilarious—Christmas, my family, the tropical paradise, the rain, everyone tiptoeing around me like I was an invalid. "Seriously, guys? Fine, I'll stop. There's no service anyway."

The bartender had indeed disappeared again, and as time passed, my dark humor blanched into a feeling of incredible nothingness. Not numbness, just nothing, anywhere, for miles around. My phone lay silent as well.

Any holiday in Puerto Rico is a good occasion for fireworks, apparently. That night at the Rincón Beach Resort, the sky came alive with them, like small explosions of mercy. Because we were on the sparsely inhabited west coast, absent were the familiar honking and screaming we would have heard in my mother-in-law's condo just outside of San Juan. We were secluded, incubated in an alternate tropical world that sent out streaking flames of celebration everywhere I turned. *He's alive! He's alive! He's alive!* they seemed to say, over and over, so that the phrase eventually lost all its meaning and became just a wave among the others, lapping up to the deserted beach.

Forgive Me

Caroline Wolff

I **SET HIM UP. I HAD PROMISED TO MEET HIM** for breakfast the next morning. In the throes of a mania so severe that it directed nearly all his actions, he somehow loved or trusted me enough to override his manic thinking and keep our breakfast date.

When the knock came on his door that morning before breakfast, it wasn't me. It was the police. They had come to take him to a psychiatric hospital. He had told me he preferred not to go to the hospital; he had asked for more time to consider treatment options. I didn't listen. After I called the police, I stayed far away. I made no attempt to see him. I sat outside the hospital on a curb, too afraid to face what was inside.

Several months later, a scene in a movie triggered thoughts of that day, and I began to cry. My husband guided me into the backseat of our car, where my crying intensified and spun out of control. I wiped at my face until my right hand became coated with mucus, thinned by tears and webbing the spaces between my fingers. He cupped my hand and clumsily flattened it against his lap, running it down the length of his thigh. "Here," he said. "This is where we wipe our nose." He didn't recoil; he didn't distract me; he didn't tell me everything was OK when it wasn't. Instead, he sat quietly and streaked his jeans with my hand, over and over. It was a gesture that convinced me that whenever I chose to leave that backseat, I could manage what came next.

The following day, I reread Leo Tolstoy's short story "The Death of Ivan Ilyich." In the story, a servant named Gerasim comforts a dying man throughout the particular horrors of his death. Gerasim is bright and cheerful and strong. He dresses neatly and smells good, like the outdoors. He doesn't shirk from emptying the chamber pot. He holds Ivan Ilyich's legs because the dying man feels better when he holds them. Gerasim accepts the ugliness of wretched illness and offers what he can to ease it because he would hope, he says, that someone will do the same for him one day. The only moments of comfort the dying man has are when Gerasim is there.

I wish that on the day the police came, I had dressed practically but respectfully: a white button-up shirt and jeans; brown boots; a sensible, pretty watch; rose perfume—the scent the strongest woman I know wears. I wish I'd waited outside and averted my eyes at the exact moment the patient was brought out of his room. I wish I had ridden with him in the fenced-in backseat of the cop car: not staring, not pitying, not chattering nervously. Just sitting quietly, perhaps putting out my hand, now and then, to touch his arm. I wish I had walked beside him into the lobby of the hospital. Perhaps the patient would not have wanted me there. Perhaps the police would have refused to allow me to be there. But I had been too scared even to ask. So again, I will borrow from Tolstoy's story and end, as he does, with this: "Forgive me."

About the Contributors

Rebecca College is a freelance writer who focuses on architecture, design, and regional development. A glass artist and sculptor in a past life, her current creative endeavor consists of making babies, a craft she feels she is on her way to mastering. She lives with her still-growing family in Pittsburgh's North Side, where she and her husband have spent the past seven years renovating their old Victorian home.

Born in Washington, DC, **Tahirah Alexander Green** currently resides in Pittsburgh, where she serves as a Compass AmeriCorps member. She graduated from Carnegie Mellon University in May 2013 with a BA in creative writing and a BS in international relations and politics. When not providing supportive services to refugees, she spends her time binging on comics and making fruit smoothies.

Lee Gutkind (editor) is the author or editor of numerous books about the medical and mental health communities, including *Many Sleepless Nights: The World of Organ Transplantation*; *Stuck in Time: The Tragedy of Childhood Mental Illness*; and *One Children's Place: Inside a Children's Hospital*. His essays about mental illness and related issues have appeared in the *New York Times* and on National Public Radio. He is the founding editor of *Creative Nonfiction* magazine and the Distinguished Writer in Residence at the Consortium for Science, Policy, and Outcomes at Arizona State University.

Yona Harvey is the author of the poetry collection *Hemming the Water*, winner of Claremont Graduate University's 2014 Kate Tufts Discovery Award. She is the recipient of an Individual Artist Grant in literary nonfiction from The Pittsburgh Foundation, and lives with her family in Pittsburgh where the neighborhoods of East Liberty, Highland Park, and Stanton Heights kiss. She is an assistant professor of English at the University of Pittsburgh, and her website is yonaharvey.com.

A native of the Midwest, **Zoë Hooley** relocated to Pittsburgh with a posse of friends and their small media company, where she works as the executive administrator and resident paperclip curator. She lives in the neighborhood of Bloomfield with her devoted puppy, Weatherby, who consumes much of her time and all of her shoes.

Andrea Laurion is a writer, improviser, and performer. Her writing has appeared in such places as the Rumpus, McSweeney's, Forbes.com, the Toast, and the *New Yinzer*, among others.

Matthew Newton is a writer and journalist from western Pennsylvania. He has written essays, many about class and culture, for *Guernica*, *Oxford American*, and the Rumpus, and his reporting has appeared in the *Atlantic*, *Esquire*, *Forbes*, and *Spin*. He is currently at work on a memoir.

Mary Elizabeth Rauktis is a native of the city of Pittsburgh, a graduate of the University of Pittsburgh, and a professor in the School of Social Work at Pitt. She has published primarily in social work and sociology journals, and has authored chapters in edited books in child welfare and in mental health. This essay was her first foray into creative nonfiction.

Linda K. Schmitmeyer is a freelance writer and editor who lives with her husband, Steve, in western Pennsylvania; they have three adult children. A former journalist, PR professional, and English teacher, she is writing a memoir about her family's experience living with Steve's mental illness.

Joni Schwager has been the executive director of the Staunton Farm Foundation since 1998. The Foundation's focus is on rural behavioral health, decriminalizing mental illness, and improving access to behavioral health care in underserved populations. Joni received her MSW from the University of Pittsburgh. During her career, she has worked in clinical, supervisory, administrative, EAP, and managed care settings.

Lauren Shapiro holds degrees from Brown University and the Iowa Writers' Workshop. She is the author of the poetry collection *Easy Math* (Sarabande Books, 2013) and a chapbook of poetry, *Yo-Yo Logic* (DIAGRAM/New Michigan Press, 2012), and she served as co-editor of The New Census: An Anthology of Contemporary American Poetry (Rescue Press, 2013). She teaches in the Creative Writing Program at Carnegie Mellon University.

Chad Vogler (co-editor) is a graduate of the MFA program at the University of Pittsburgh and has been an assistant editor at the Creative Nonfiction Foundation since 2012.

After writing about current events for *Foreign Policy* and *Slate* magazines in Washington, DC, **Caroline Wolff** came to the University of Pittsburgh's MFA program in nonfiction to learn to write about psychology. Her next project looks at the psychology of hiking the Pacific Crest Trail—a 2663-mile, five-month walk through the mountains of California, Oregon, and Washington—in one go.

39704611R00058

Made in the USA
Charleston, SC
14 March 2015